Oneness With God

Biblical References are from the King James Version. Special acknowledgement is made to the King James Study Bible by Thomas Nelson Publishers.

Published in the United States by
Beckham Publications Group, Inc.
P.O. Box 4066, Silver Spring, MD 20914

Library of Congress Control Number: 2006926331

ISBN: 0-931761-39-5

Oneness With God

A Christian Attorney's Analysis of What It Means to be Created in the Image and After the Likeness of God

Ronald E. Richardson

THE **Beckham**
PUBLICATIONS GROUP, INC.
Silver Spring

CONTENTS

FOREWORD

Throughout the course of recorded history, Man, as a relational being, has grappled with the origin and nature of his existence and its impact on that of others. Central to this investigatory reflection and the resultant research has been the inherently compelling need to understand Man's relationship with God and even to know the very nature of God Himself. But God is Spirit and those who seek Him must do so through the spiritual realm.

In his quest to "know," Man must also acknowledge that he is fearfully and wonderfully made in the image of an invisible, holy God. He who seeks to ferret out the essence of God and His divine intention relative to sinful Man must begin at the point of creation. In the beginning, God so loved the world that He gave His only begotten Son. The foundational principle of God's relationship with Man is love. The begotten Son so loved His father that He endured the death of the cross that Man might return to Genesis, to the beginning. Any Man who seeks God's grace and confesses his sin is privileged to experience a relationship with God, to know the heart of God and to know God's desire for the life of the believer The essence of all human relationships is inextricably intertwined with Man's relationship with God and God's love for Man.

Oneness with God represents just such an intentional seeking to understand the nature of God and his purposed relationship to Man, his creation. Richardson's writing reflects the work of a transformed Man panting after the heart of God, searching for the keys to a genuine relationship with God through a relationship with His Son. This writer uses his "trained mind" and his personal experiences to interpret God's divine purpose for believers. He informs us that God created the world with His faith and that believers do indeed have that same creative faith which they should engage to live in oneness with God.

Yes, believers certainly do have that same faith because of God's prophetic intention. *Oneness with God* is indeed a reflection of His prophetic intention in the life of every believer. By faith, the principle of equivalent effect helps us to evangelize others to receive that word of oneness spoken originally. Richardson captures John chapter seventeen from an analytical mind set with a passion for the spiritual. This book is a must read!

Pastor Clifford M. Johnson, Jr.

PROLOGUE

The phrase "Christian attorney" has been viewed by some to be an oxymoron of sorts. Many people think that attorneys will do whatever it takes to win for their clients even if it means violating the laws of God. Furthermore, a lawyer's interpretation of the law typically does not allow for concepts such as forgiveness or grace. Perhaps this is why those law experts of Jesus' day, the Pharisees, could not bring themselves to accept His gospel of grace, forgiveness and redemption. Christians, however, have surrendered their entire lives to Jesus Christ in the faith that His death and resurrection have freed them from the wages of their sins and, by grace, granted them eternal salvation. Christians, in fact, are allowed to fulfill their creative purpose, which is to become one with God.

It would appear, then, that it would be extremely difficult for an attorney to be a Christian. However, just as Paul, a legal expert and a Pharisee, was won over to Christ, attorneys can likewise be called by God to accept Jesus Christ as their Lord and Savior. I know from experience. Jesus Christ is my Lord and Savior, and I am a lawyer.

My Loyola Law School degree and almost two decades of legal practice have trained me to appreciate the importance of detail and choosing the right words to convey the exact message intended. When briefing an issue before a court of law, the extent to which a lawyer possesses these talents will determine whether or not the court will agree with his interpretation of the law. This book does not address the ethical or moral issues surrounding a lawyer's interpretation of man's or God's law for the benefit of a client. Rather, it is an attempt to strictly construe the passages of the Bible, from the perspective of a lawyer, to determine the intent of God with respect to why He created mankind.

If ever there is a written work where the meaning of every word is critical to an understanding of the message contained therein, the Holy Scriptures, which are inspired by God, is such a work. Any analysis thereof will necessarily require an occasional review of the original text or a comparison of various translations. We must operate on the premise that every word contained therein was specifically chosen to convey this wonderful gospel—"the Good News".

By the guidance of the Holy Spirit, this book presents an analysis of the Holy Scriptures in an attempt to shed some light upon the mystery behind the creation of man in the image and after the likeness of God and the awesome role we are to play in God's order of things. From the dawn of history to the present, man has striven to become God. Either he seeks to become the master of his own destiny or he seeks to exercise godlike powers over others, or both. This innate desire of man to become God can be traced back to the beginning, to the creation of man.

Mankind was made in the image and after the likeness of God, that is, given the appearance, attributes, characteristics, and mannerisms of God so that we can be perfect temples, individually and collectively, for our Holy God. Essentially, we were created to become the physical manifestations of God to the same extent that Jesus is the embodiment of God. Most Christian denominations today do not teach of us becoming one with our Creator perhaps because of a concern of being viewed as advocating our elevation to the likeness of God. But this is exactly what the Holy Scriptures state is the creative purpose for mankind.

Satan understood this all too well and risked certain eternal damnation by seeking to contravene God's plan for us and by exciting a physical and spiritual rebellion against God. The opportunity presented itself to Satan when God decided to determine the extent of man's love for Him through the test of obedience. With a little help from Satan, Adam and Eve, our first parents, failed this test. The consequences of their sin of disobedience required not only their deaths through eternal separation from God but also the same fate for all of their offspring. However, God allowed a part of Himself to become man, through the person of Jesus Christ, and pay the wages of the sins of us all by suffering the most brutal and horrific scourging any man will ever have to endure for sins that He did not commit. Thereby we were redeemed and restored to an existence that will allow us to perform that holy purpose for which we were created, as set forth in 2 Corinthians 6:16-18:

> And what agreement hath the temple of God with idols? for ye are the temple of the living God; as God hath said, I WILL DWELL IN THEM, AND WALK IN THEM; AND I WILL BE THEIR GOD, AND THEY SHALL BE MY PEOPLE.
>
> Wherefore, COME OUT FROM AMONG THEM, AND BE YE SEPARATE, saith the Lord, AND TOUCH NOT THE UNCLEAN THING; AND I WILL RECEIVE YOU,
>
> AND WILL BE A FATHER UNTO YOU, AND YE SHALL BE MY SONS AND DAUGHTERS, saith the Lord Almighty.

If we use nothing more than our God-given common sense, we must conclude that, as the reborn children of God, we are His offspring and thereby possess the same spiritual characteristics and attributes as God, our Father. Jesus is the perfect example of who we were created to be. However, the life of Jesus demonstrates a caveat to us fulfilling our creative purpose. We must be submissive to the will of God to the same extent that Jesus submitted to God's will. We must strive to be the least in the Kingdom of God in order to be the greatest. By this I mean that we must completely submit ourselves to the will of God, even unto death, because it is through this uncompromising obedience to God that we demonstrate our unconditional love for Him and can become one with Him. He demonstrated the same unconditional love for us when He sacrificed His only begotten Son for our salvation.

As children of God called to become one with Him, we eagerly await the day when Jesus returns so that we may be glorified into His mirror image and can live and reign with Him forever. Our spiritual rebirths and ultimate glorification will perfect our personal and collective oneness with God.

From the moment of my spiritual rebirth, which occurred during the third year of my four-year evening law school program, I have asked God to explain, to the satisfaction of my soul, why He allowed a part of Himself to suffer and die for the sins of man? I knew the boiler-plate responses to that question that have rolled off the tongues of Christians for two millennia. However, I felt in my heart that there was more to this story. So I undertook to satisfy my appetite for the truth, the whole truth, and nothing but the truth concerning the reason for God's ultimate sacrifice for man.

As I delved into the Word of God in my quest to answer this fundamental question, I began to conceptualize God's creative purpose for man. The more I learned, the more wondrous and awesome the answer became. I was so taken by the profoundness of God's creative purpose for every human being, as revealed to me through the Word of God, that I felt compelled to write this book. I pray that I have been able to articulate the magnitude of the answer to this age-old question in such a way that any reader hereof will fully grasp its significance and revel in the indescribable joy, peace, and wonderment that comes with its understanding.

This book discusses the nature and extent of our oneness with God which is exactly like the relationship Jesus enjoys as God and yet as the human Son of God. Indeed, Jesus is the firstborn of all the children of God. God's greatest creation, humankind, was always intended to become one with God to the same extent that Jesus is one with Him. Just the thought of being one with God to this extent is overwhelming. Yet this awesome reality is set forth in the Word of God, which is alive, true, and sure and indeed is a revelation and expression of God Himself.

God's Holy Word says that "EYE HATH NOT SEEN, NOR EAR HEARD, NEITHER HAVE ENTERED INTO THE HEART OF MAN, THE THINGS WHICH GOD HATH PREPARED FOR THEM THAT LOVE HIM" (1 Corinthians 2:9). As we currently exist, we cannot know the mind of God. As we will exist, we shall not only know the mind of God but shall also share the mind of God. Jesus prayed that we be one with God just as He is one with God. Jesus knew the mind of God. If we are to be one with God at Jesus' level, then we shall come to know all things about God.

This book will provide, through the trained eye of a literalist, a glimpse into the will of God contained in the Word of God as it relates to why God created us in His image and after His likeness. Just as a lawyer would cite the legal basis contained in the law for any supposition or conclusion he might make, we shall review the biblical support for the gospel of Jesus Christ because it is inextricably connected with the creative purpose of man. Through the ensuing chapters, we shall examine why I believe that God created mankind to become one with Him; man's failure of God's test of obedience and Satan's role in it; God's redemption of man; man's spiritual rebirth; and, finally, the perfection of God's creative purpose for mankind. The story of man in God's master plan has been told innumerable times. This book focuses on God's purpose behind the story.

It is my fervent prayer that this book will explain the gospel of Jesus Christ and the master plan of God for us in a way that the reborn children of God will be strengthened and encouraged to finish the race knowing that their glorified states will mirror Jesus in every respect. This book is also written for all those who have yet to accept the free gift of eternal salvation through Jesus Christ, in the hope that, with a better appreciation of who they really are and why they exist, they will understand why Jesus is the only way to eternal life and oneness with God.

Understanding the big picture helps us to better deal with the day-to-day challenges of our spiritual walk with God. Praise be to God for choosing to restore us to our original estate and allowing us to house His spiritual essence and to thereby experience Him in a way that cannot now be imagined. May God open our spiritual eyes and ears and grant us the wisdom to understand the fullness of His purpose for our creation in His image and after His likeness.

CHAPTER ONE

GOD'S MASTER PLAN—
THE BEGINNING

A ny good story is most effectively told when it is started from the beginning. Therefore we shall begin the eternal story of God's master plan to create a perfect universe, which would be ruled by Him as one with man, His highest creation, by examining the creation process itself.

God's plan for all creation, including our roles in it, was conceived by God before the foundation of the world. The concept of time did not exist before the beginning; time was introduced when God created the heavens and the earth. God, in His omniscience, saw all things that will occur from the beginning of time to the end of time. He is, after all, the Alpha and the Omega and is not constrained by time. All was known by God before the beginning. The initiation of time by God started the replay of a story already told; one whose storyline and ending is known only by the author thereof.

God intended no other created thing or being to have

significance greater than that of mankind because man was created to be one with his Creator. Man's creative purpose so interconnects him with all of physical creation that, when Adam and Eve sinned, everything in the physical realm also began to die with them (Romans 8:18-22). As a result, God initiated a master plan that, over the course of time, was designed to restore mankind and the physical realm to their original state of perfection.

In this chapter, we shall first consider the role each of the three personages of our triune Godhead played in the creation process. We shall then attempt to view creation from both God's eternal perspective and our earthly perspective. Finally, we shall discuss the role that faith has played in the creation of all things, and the role it continues to play in the effectuation of God's master plan to become one with us. The evidence set forth below points to but one inescapable conclusion, and that is that all of creation, both physical and spiritual, were created by and for the benefit of God.

The Triune Godhead in Creation

The Bible states that "In the beginning God created the heaven and the earth" (Genesis 1:1). The Hebrew word for God used in this text is *Elohim*, which is a plural form of the divine name signifying the existence of God the Father, His Living Word, and the Holy Spirit. This triune Godhead, composed of three separate, equal persons, is at the same time one deity, who is God. This is corroborated by the Apostle John, who wrote, "For there are three that bear record in heaven, the Father, the Word, and the Holy Ghost: and these three are one" (1 John 5:7).

Next, consider what Matthew was inspired to write. He said that Jesus sent His disciples into the world to teach all nations and baptize them "in the name of the Father, and of the Son, and of the Holy Ghost" (Matthew 28:19). Notice that the use of the word "name" is singular. This demonstrates that this triune Godhead is one in every respect; so much so that a single name is used to refer to all three of them. In Isaiah 6:2-3, we discover that the seraphim cry praises to each other declaring "Holy, holy, holy, is the LORD of hosts". Again, the word "Lord" is singular. This threefold declaration is for the threefold personages of God. In a later chapter, I discuss those passages of the Bible which establish that all of the children of God adopt the same name as that of our triune Godhead. This is God's affirmation that He intends for us to be one with Him in every respect.

In looking again at the Genesis creation account, we find that the Hebrew word for "created" is *bara*. It is a singular verb used with a plural noun *Elohim* (Genesis 1:1). What does this indicate? It is further confirmation of both the plurality and oneness of our triune Godhead.

Psalm 33:6 states: "By the word of the LORD were the heavens made; and all the host of them by the breath of his mouth". Second Peter 3:5 echoes this fact by stating, "by the word of God the heavens were of old, and the earth standing out of the water and in the water." Indeed, when one looks at the creation passages contained in Genesis 1, every phase of creation begins with the phrase "And God said". Psalm 148:1-6 command us to praise the Lord, for He created all things in heaven and on earth and established them forever by making a decree that shall not pass. That decree was an oral one.

One may ask "Who is this spoken Word of God?" The answer to this question is revealed in the Holy Scriptures, which tell us that Jesus Christ is the Word of God (Luke 8:11; John 1:1, 14; Revelation 19:13). This begs the questions "How could the Son of God, Who was born thousands of years after Adam, participate in creation week as the Living Word of God?" and "How can we rationalize this if we interpret these passages literally?" From a strict constructionist point of view, the references to Jesus Christ as the Word of God in the Holy Scriptures demand but one conclusion: that Jesus is the *literal* Word of God Who was made flesh and dwelt among us as the only begotten Son of God. Jesus is the embodiment of every utterance from God. It is interesting to note that several translations of Genesis 3:8 state that Adam and Eve heard the voice of God walking in the garden. This would be none other than the pre-incarnate Jesus. Jesus is also the written Word of God since all Scriptures are inspired by God, the Holy Spirit. The Scriptures are alive with the presence of Jesus Christ, both in and of them. In Jesus dwells all the fullness of the Godhead bodily (Colossians 2:9).

As the eternal Living Word of God, Jesus is both one and equal to God the Father and God the Holy Spirit. John 1:1-3 confirm the oneness between God and Jesus:

> In the beginning was the Word, and the Word was with God, and the Word was God.The same was in the beginning with God. All things were made by him; and without him was not any thing made that was made.

However, when Jesus became the Son of God, He subjected Himself to the authority of God the Father

(John 14:28; 1 Corinthians 15:27-28).

The Holy Spirit was also intricately involved in the creation process, when He hovered over the face of the waters (Genesis 1:2) and adorned the heavens (Job 26:13). He continues to renew the earth and everything in it (Psalms 104:30). Thus, all three persons of the Godhead were involved in creation week (Genesis 1:1-2; John 1:3).

Creation and Evolution

A brief discussion about creation versus evolution, with respect to the physical realm, is warranted. The question about whether mankind, the earth and, indeed, the universe are the result of a supernatural creation process completed over a period of six days or an evolutionary process spanning millions, if not billions, of years is unequivocally answered in the first chapter of the book of Genesis. In Genesis 1:5, God defines the first day as being an evening and a morning. In fact, God attributes so much importance to this definition of a day that He ends each day's work with the same definition of a day (Genesis 1:5, 8, 13, 19, 23, 31). Obviously, God sought to drive home the point that He accomplished the creation of the physical realm in six literal days.

The Bible does not explain how God performed this supernatural feat. For that matter, it doesn't explain how any of the miracles of our triune Godhead were accomplished. We will most likely never fully understand the mechanics behind the wondrous works of God until we are glorified in Christ Jesus upon His return.

What the Bible does tell us is that one day to the

Lord is as a thousand years, and a thousand years as one day (2 Peter 3:8). The first half of this verse could be interpreted to mean that each day is as an infinity to God because a thousand years are composed of hundreds of thousands of days; each of which is like a thousand years that, together, consists of millions of days; each of which is like a thousand years, and so forth. Based upon our interpretation of the first half of this verse, the second part of this verse would necessarily mean that, from God's perspective, infinity can occur in the span of one day. This would be consistent with Genesis 5:1-2 wherein God tells us that the creation of mankind was accomplished "in the day" as opposed to "on the day." In other words, since God is the Beginning and the End and does not reside in this temporal existence of ours, He can supernaturally cram hundreds of millions of years into the span of one week. With God, all things are possible (Matthew 19:26).

Evolutionists cannot accept such an interpretation because it defies "science" and requires a leap of faith. This is a bit ironic since, as we shall see, faith is exactly what the Holy Scriptures say God used to form all of creation from things that are unseen.

The Role of Faith in the Creation Process

We know that God is faithful (1 Corinthians 1:9; 1 Thessalonians 5:24; 2 Thessalonians 3:3). The question is, what is faith? According to Hebrews 11:1, faith is defined as "the substance of things hoped for, the evidence of things not seen." The Greek word for "substance," in this context, is *hypostasis*, which means "assurance, confidence or realization." This is to be distinguished from the Greek word *hyparxis*, which is often used for the word "substance" and means "possessions or property, wealth, or goods." Therefore faith is the assurance or confidence that unseen things, which are hoped for, will be realized. This verse helps us to understand how all things were created from nothing. It took God's matchless faith to bring into realization every created thing, both physical and spiritual.

It may be difficult for some to comprehend how God's faith can perform, from that which is unseen, such feats as the realization of His spiritual kingdom, an entire universe, and all that is in it. However, the Holy Scriptures are replete with instances in which faith is the underlying source for the performance of wondrous miracles of healing and deliverance. During His earthly ministry, Jesus placed heavy emphasis on the power of faith.

As we look further at Genesis 1:1 we find that the Hebrew word for "heaven" is *shamayim,* the root of which is *shameh,* which means "heaven seen and unseen." This suggests that all things, visible and invisible, were created "in the beginning." This includes all matter, from huge planets to microscopic atoms, molecules, or particles. It also includes all things spiritual, such as the angels. This is confirmed in Colossians 1:16-17 which state

> For by him were all things created, that are in heaven, and that are in earth, visible and invisible, whether they be thrones, or dominions, or principalities, or powers: all things were created by him, and for him: And he is before all things, and by him all things consist.

God's faith is absolute and limitless. It is so sure that

it is, for all practical purposes, actual knowledge. With this kind of faith, God can realize and sustain anything.

God demonstrated His faithfulness in a mighty way during creation week. When God said "Let there be light" (Genesis 1:3), His living words were able to effectuate his command because of the power attendant with His limitless faith.

Hebrews 11:3 tells us that

> Through faith we understand that the worlds were framed by the word of God, so that things which are seen were not made of things which do appear.

Thus, faith is the only means by which the unseen can be realized (Hebrews 11:1). Indeed, this degree of faith cannot be fully appreciated by man. To create the universe and all that is in it, with the intricate order and arrangement of it all, takes a great and intelligent mind beyond our imagination, with faith too powerful and awesome to describe. Without our triune God's faith the universe would not exist; and through this limitless faith the universe consists, that is, holds together. The Bible tells us that God upholds all things by the word of His power (Hebrews 1:3). The power of our faithful God manifests itself through Jesus Christ, His spoken word.

Also, because God is always the same yesterday, today, and forever, His level of faithfulness never decreases; and all that He has made to be realized will always exist in the form He wills it to be (Hebrews 13:8; Malachi 3:6).

The Role of Faith in God's Master Plan for Man

Acceptance of what the Bible says about the role God's faith played in the creation process requires faith on the part of the child of God. Indeed, in His eternal master plan for mankind, God intends that faith play an equally vital role in the life and salvation of each of His children. The apostle Paul informs us in Romans 1:20 that

> For the invisible things of him from the creation of the world are clearly seen, being understood by the things that are made, even his eternal power and Godhead; so that they are without excuse.

The context of this verse is that our invisible God is revealed to every one of us through all of creation, which can be clearly seen. However, it requires faith for us to see that the world and everything in it is a revelation of God's eternal power and divine nature.

No man has ever mastered faith to the extent that God has. However, in our soon-to-be-glorified states, when we are one with Him, our mastery of faith will allow us to create and sustain to the same extent that God can. This is only possible because God will be so much a part of us that His faith will become our faith, His will our will.

The writer of the book of Hebrews introduces the definition of faith with the word "Now." There has been much discussion as to what meaning the writer of Hebrews intended for the word "Now" in this verse. It could serve equally as well as an adverb, conjunction, noun, adjective, or interjection. Let's look at the possibilities. As an adverb, the word "Now" would mean "at the present time," "at this moment," or "at once." This passage, then, would mean that the faith one currently possesses is the substance of things hoped for. The word "Now" could serve as a conjunction, thus connecting the message of chapter 10 of Hebrews to that of chapter 11. The message of chapter 10 is that Christ's once-for-all sacrifice has replaced the old covenant's yearly animal sacrifice, thereby allowing all who believe in faith to have direct access to the throne of God. The message of chapter 11 is that true faith is the means of realizing the promises of the new covenant.

As a noun, the word "Now" would simply mean "the present time." As an adjective, it would mean "of the present time." Finally, as an interjection, it would signify a preface or resumption of the writer's previous remarks.

Could it not be that the writer of Hebrews intended for the word "Now" to function in *each* of these ways simultaneously? You see, the word "Now" introduces and connects the most important word, "faith." In other words, the faith that each child of God possesses concerning his or her salvation through Jesus Christ is the means through which his or her salvation will be realized. They abide in God, and He in them. His faith becomes their faith. With the faith of God, all things are possible because there is no limit to His faith.

The apostle Paul wrote: "Faithful is he that calleth you, who also will do it" (1 Thessalonians 5:24). We were predestined before the foundation of the world to be heirs of salvation and fellow brethren of Jesus Christ. Our God, Who is faithful, will make this a realization. Whoever is born of God overcomes the world, and the victory that overcomes the world is our faith (1 John 5:4). Scripture reminds us that we are saved by the hope of what is not seen; and we patiently wait for it (Romans 8:24-25).

Now then, since faith is the realization of things

hoped for, anything we ask of God, whether it be as intercessors for others or on our own behalf, must first be hoped for, and we must wait patiently for it to be realized. The faith of God, who lives in and through us, will bring it to realization. This is why we walk by faith and not by sight (2 Corinthians 5:7). This faith comes by hearing, and hearing by the Word of God (Romans 10:17). It is the faith of God by and through which our salvation can be assured. Since God is the author of our salvation, according to Hebrews 5:9, His limitless faith will ensure that we are indeed saved.

As the children of God, we are of one faith. For it is written in Ephesians 4:4-6:

> There is one body, and one Spirit, even as ye are
> called in one hope of your calling; One Lord,
> one faith, one baptism, One God and Father of all,
> who is above all, and through all, and in you all.

We therefore must be very careful of what we say when we are in the Spirit; because when we speak, our faithful God, Who in-dwells us, lives in our words and, therefore, they have power. With God in us and we in Him, we can tell a mountain to remove to another place, and it will do it. Nothing shall be impossible for us (Matthew 17:20).

The Scriptures warn us not to let any corrupt communications proceed out of our mouths but only that which is good for teaching, so that it may minister grace unto the hearers (Ephesians 4:29). We are told in Proverbs 14:5 that a faithful witness will not lie. In James 3:8-10, we are cautioned to be careful with our tongue, lest we curse men who are made after the likeness of God. In other words, as we curse others, we may inadvertently curse reborn children of God who have been restored to the image and the likeness of God.

We cannot lose our salvation because we are spiritually reborn of God and therefore have His spiritual genes in us. We can no more rid ourselves of God's spiritual genes than we can the genes we are physically born with. They determine our physical and spiritual personalities and are with us for the duration of our physical and spiritual lives. The assurance of our salvation is the result of our spiritual genetic relationship with God. Thus, no one is able to pluck us out of the hand of Jesus or God the Father since They are one (John 10:25-30).

Some have cited John 15:2 to support the contention that the saved can lose their salvation. Let's carefully examine this verse:

> Every branch in me that beareth not fruit he taketh away: and every branch that beareth fruit, he purgeth it, that it may bring forth more fruit.

These words of Christ have been incorrectly interpreted to mean that the children of God, who abide in Christ and are therefore saved, will be removed from Him and, inferentially, lose their salvation if they do not bear fruit. Nothing could be further from the truth.

To clearly understand what Jesus is telling us in John 15:1-7, we need to have an appreciation of what is involved in the growing of grapes. Bruce Wilkinson, in his book *Secrets of the Vine*, gives us an excellent explanation of the process of growing grapes. He states that the vinedresser, first of all, never cuts off and discards branches that bear no fruit. Instead, he lifts the nonproductive branches off the ground; he cleans them up and secures them on the trellis, thereby enabling them to bear fruit. The King James translation of scriptures such as Matthew 14:20; 27:32; and John 1:29 lends to the mistaken interpretation of the Greek word *airo* to mean "take away." It really means "take up," "lift up," or "to bear".

Any branch (that is, believer) who is united to the true vine, Jesus, cannot be cast away. If a believer is not bearing fruit, God lifts up that child of His and cleanses that person's heart and soul so that spiritual fruit-bearing can begin. Purging is a form of pruning, oftentimes painful, that enables a branch already bearing fruit to bear even more fruit. Many servants of God, such as the Old Testament prophets and Jesus' disciples, were made to endure trying times so that they would be able to bear increasingly more spiritual fruit. It is the branches who are not connected to the vine, and therefore are not in Jesus, that are cast into the fire and burned (John 15:6). Fruit-bearing, you see, is part of the Creator's master plan for us.

The importance of faith in the life of a child of God, according to God's master plan, cannot be overstressed. The Holy Scriptures are replete with examples of the power of faith when exercised by man, causing his unseen hopes to be realized immediately or over time.

One example of the immediate realization of unseen hopes through faith was when Jesus spoke healing into the nobleman's sick son which occurred at the moment the nobleman believed Him (John 4:43-53). Another example is the unwavering faith of Joshua that allowed him to command the sun and moon to stay still for the span of one day while the Israelites defeated the Amorites (Joshua 10:12-14).

In the Acts of the Apostles, the apostle Luke describes the healing of a lame man through the apostles Peter and John:

> And his name through faith in his name hath made this man strong, whom ye see and know: yea, the faith which is by him hath given him this perfect soundness in the presence of you all. (Acts 3:16)

Peter is telling those gathered around the man who was healed that it was the man's faith in the name of Jesus that allowed the faith of Jesus to immediately make him strong.

Through faith, unseen hopes can also be realized over time, as was the case with Moses and Abraham. We are told that by faith Moses "forsook Egypt, not fearing the wrath of the king: for he endured, as seeing him who is invisible" (Hebrews 11:27). Thus, by faith we can see God, who is invisible. Jesus told us that Abraham rejoiced to see His day; and Abraham saw it and was glad (John 8:56). The only way for our father Abraham (Romans 4:1-16) to see Jesus' day was by faith through his spiritual eyes.

That is why the writer of Hebrews goes to such great lengths to testify about the power of faith in anointed people of God throughout the ages. These men and women knew that their unseen hopes would eventually be realized because of their faith in the Word of God (Hebrews 11:4-40).

The faith of our triune God, when called upon through our faith, will never fail us and will give us perfect soundness. It necessarily follows that the realization of our unseen hopes is limited only by the extent of our faith in God's faithfulness, which is determined by the extent of our intimacy and oneness with God. That, in turn, is determined by the extent of our reading of and obedience to the Word of God. The more we abide in God and He in us, the more access we have to His limitless faith.

When we ultimately attain our incorruptible states, our faith will be one and the same as God's limitless faith because of our complete oneness with Him. In such a state, all things hoped for will be realized unto the glory of God, including the literal movement of mountains. However, we do not have to wait until we are glorified with Jesus to experience God's limitless faith. As spiritually reborn children of God, we have direct access to God's limitless faith now. All we have to do is demonstrate our uncompromising and unconditional love for God by letting God live in and through us. The more we die to self, the more God lives in and through us. As a result, whatever we ask for in faithful prayer, we shall receive insofar as it is the will of God (Matthew 21:22).

He does this for us because Christ is the originator and perfecter of our faith (Hebrews 12:2). Our unseen salvation is realized, through the grace of God, by our hope and faith in the name of Christ Jesus, Who is God. Yes, we can do all things through Christ who strengthens us (Philippians 4:13). The Holy Spirit strengthens us as we eagerly wait for our hope of righteousness to be realized through faith (Galatians 5:5). Once realized, we will be like Jesus (2 Corinthians 3:18).

Because of our faith in Jesus Christ, God imputes— that is, puts into our account—the righteousness of Jesus (Romans 10:3-4; Philippians 3:9). The definition of the word "impute," as contained in Black's Law Dictionary, can be paraphrased using a Christian analogy as follows: "Righteousness is imputed to a child of God when it is ascribed or charged to him, not because he is personally cognizant of it or deserving of it, but because another is; namely, Jesus the Christ."

It is the righteousness that is imputed unto us by our faith in Christ Jesus that enables us to be transformed into the express image of Jesus, who is the express image of God. This transformation will not be totally complete until we are given our incorruptible bodies and become completely one with God, just as Jesus is one with God in glory. In the meantime, our ever-maturing faith through Christ Jesus will allow us to realize our unseen hopes; some sooner than others.

Only true faith, which stems from Jesus, can bring about the realization of the unseen hopes of every child of God who is to be glorified unto God in the image of Jesus. All other faith is vain.

And what is vain faith? Vain faith is baseless faith. In 1 Corinthians 15, the apostle Paul discusses the difference between vain, baseless faith and true faith. Vain, baseless faith is that which is not founded upon God's truth. Paul uses three Greek words to describe such baseless, vain faith. The first word is *Eikei* which means "without effect." In other words, faith without Jesus Christ cannot effectuate the realization of unseen hopes. The second word is *Kenos,* which means "without success," "without truth," and "without basis." Clearly, this kind of faith, lacking as it does any divine basis, cannot successfully realize unseen hopes. The third word the apostle uses in this chapter to describe vain faith is *Mataios,* which means "useless." This type of faith is a waste of time because it can do nothing for the believer.

Anything that is not of the limitless faith of God is sin (Romans 14:23). The devils believe that there is one God (James 2:19), but they will never realize their unseen hopes of usurping God's authority and ruling the heavens and the earth in His stead because their faith is not grounded in the Word of God. Clearly, it is impossible for the unseen hopes of a faithless person to be realized. Baseless, vain faith cannot bring about the realization of unseen hopes.

There is only one true faith, and the only source of that faith is our triune Godhead (Ephesians 4:4-6). We can be faithful only because God is faithful. We comprise the spiritual Body of Christ, who is the faithful witness (Revelation 1:5, 3:14). If we ask anything of God, in faith, wavering not, it shall be given unto us (James 1:5-6). However, we should only ask for unseen hopes that are in furtherance of God's holy will. The realization of these hopes would then be the effectuation of His perfect will to His honor and glory.

True faith is demonstrated through the fruits of our faith by our works. True faith works not for salvation, but because of salvation. The works, which are the consequence of true faith, do not bring about salvation. Instead, they are the natural and practical result of salvation.

James, the brother of Jesus, tells us that just as the body without the spirit is dead, so faith without works is dead (James 2:26). He writes:

> What doth it profit, my brethren, though a man say he hath faith, and have not works? can faith save him? Even so faith, if it hath not works, is dead, being alone. (James 2:14, 17)

According to James, in order for faith to have any effect, the believer must be willing to engage in acts in furtherance of his acknowledged faith. This is the fruit-bearing I referred to earlier. Jesus once said "According to your faith be it unto you" (Matthew 9:29). It was faith in the underlying faithfulness of Jesus that formed the basis for His miraculous ministry. Jesus taught with authority (Matthew 7:29). He gives this same authority to those who believe in Him in faith. For instance, He gave it to His disciples (Luke 9:1), and they were able to exercise this God-given authority according to the measure of their faith (Mark 9: 14-29).

The apostle Paul asserts that the members of the Body of Christ have been given measures of faith proportionally through Jesus Christ according to the determined grace of God (Romans12:3-8). Jesus Christ is the source of all grace and faith, which He distributes proportionately to His brethren according to God's good pleasure. In a later chapter, we will discuss how the children of God, being members of the spiritual Body of Christ, have different functions requiring varying levels of faith and suffering, just as the physical members of Jesus' body had different functions and levels of suffering. The measure of faith given and the degree of suffering attributed to every member of the spiritual Body of Christ is determined by the specific function each member is asked to perform.

Every child of God, being a member of the Body of Christ, has the faithfulness of God living in him and through him. We are one in body, spirit, hope, and faith; yet every one of us has differing gifts to be used according to the proportion of faith given to us by Jesus Christ (Ephesians 4:4-7). It is the oneness of our collective faith, which is the faith of God, that ensures our salvation and the realization of all that is promised to us as heirs of salvation.

Faith, you see, is extremely important in the life of a believer. It allows us to use our spiritual senses and gifts. According to Jesus, that's why He used parables. Those who have no faith will hear these parables and yet not hear; they will see and yet not see. They will not understand with their heart. However, blessed are our eyes for they see, and our ears, for they hear (Matthew 13:10-17). Faith opens our spiritual eyes and ears. It causes us to understand the Word of God.

Envision, if you will, that every human being has a life car that proceeds down the road of life until the fuel runs out. From birth we are taught that we have to learn how to drive that car and eventually to take control of our life car's steering wheel so that we can maneuver our way through our respective courses of life. Since everyone wants to be in control of their own lives, we instinctively balk at the thought of letting someone else drive our life cars.

When we accept the death and resurrection of our Lord and Savior Jesus Christ for the forgiveness of our sins and the salvation of our souls, in faith, and are thereby spiritually reborn, we relinquish control of the steering wheels to our life cars and give them over to our invisible God. We do so because we trust in His Word that, with Him behind our steering wheels, we shall never run out of fuel and He will direct our paths.

Now our jobs and worldly possessions are in that car. For those of us who have families, our families are in the back seat. It takes a leap of faith to move over to the passenger seat and let our invisible God drive our life cars, especially when we see life's stop signs, turns, traffic, potholes and the like directly in our paths.

As our invisible God begins to drive our life cars, we nervously gaze with our earthly eyes at what appears to be an empty driver's seat. Every bone in our bodies anticipates a wreck with potential fatalities. We instinctively want to snatch control of that steering wheel and rely on what we can physically see instead of on what we cannot physically see (faith).

However, the faith of God, Who is the author and finisher of our faith, abides in us and keeps us still. The more we observe Him weaving in and out of traffic, avoiding the potholes, and otherwise being true to His Word, our faith matures and we are at peace. When non-believers observe us safely proceeding through life, content and at peace in the passenger seats of our life cars without any apparent driver behind the steering wheel, they marvel at our ability to stay on course. They question the source of our remarkable faith and say to themselves that there must be something to this invisible God of ours. Hopefully, they will be encouraged to similarly relieve themselves of the stress and burden of driving their life cars until the fuel is depleted or they wreck and turn that responsibility over to God, Who promises that the fuel will never run dry and that our life cars will always remain on course—His course.

As the faithfulness of our triune Godhead becomes our faithfulness, we develop into illuminating lights of varying degrees in this otherwise dark world. We allow the lost to see that, through the death and resurrection of the Word of God, our Lord Jesus Christ, salvation is at hand for all who are willing to accept it on their behalf through faith.

Once our faith endures to the end, we shall eat of the Tree of Life, as we were originally intended to do (Revelation 2:7). It is crucial that we understand the importance of faith, not just in the redemption of mankind, but in God's original master plan for man, conceived before the beginning and put into effect at Creation.

According to the order of things as determined by God in the beginning, the chosen people of God, who are spiritually begotten of Him, will become mirror images of Jesus. We will abide in Him and He will abide in us. When He is seen; we are seen; and when we are seen, He is seen. That is why God sees Jesus when He looks at His spiritually reborn children who comprise the spiritual Body of Christ. Since God's definition of "righteous" is Jesus Christ, we are righteous before His eyes because Jesus is righteous.

In *Webster's New World Dictionary,* "righteous" is defined as "acting in a just, upright manner; doing what is right, virtuous; morally right, fair and just." In a legal context, "righteous" means obeying the law; free from blame. Any transgression of man's law requires a penalty to be paid that is commensurate to the severity of the transgression. Any act in violation of God's law, regardless of severity, requires the same penalty: death through eternal damnation and separation from God.

Because of our sin nature, passed down to every person born of Adam, no person can be righteous under God's law. Jesus, not having Adam's sin nature, being born of God, remained obedient to God and therefore was righteous throughout His earthly life. He gave up His life so that we would not have to, though our transgressions demanded our deaths and eternal separations from God. He voluntarily paid God's penalty for the sins of the world. The only requirement is that we accept His sacrifice on our behalf in the faith that God will deliver on His promise of eternal salvation. Incredibly, many refuse to do so. Instead, they choose to find their own way to eternal life just as Adam did. All who accept Jesus' sacrifice on their behalf take on the image and likeness of Jesus; become righteous before God, and have eternal life. All who do not accept Jesus' sacrifice are eternally damned. Jesus is the firstborn and the head of a spiritual body composed of those who were made righteous because of their acceptance of His blameless death on their behalf. Once we take on His image and likeness, we become one with Him. Since there is no limit to what Jesus can do, there is no limit to what we, who are one with Him, can do. Our imaginations cannot begin to see what glorious things we can accomplish now and when we are completely one with God, as we were originally intended to be before the beginning.

It is often asked, when shall our glorification with God occur? This same question was asked of Jesus by His disciples. The apostle Matthew, in chapter 24 of his book, transcribes Jesus' response to this question. He identifies the signs of the times that are associated with His return and our glorification in and through Him. Many biblical scholars believe that we are living in the days during which these signs are occurring. With every passing day, there is an on-going polarization between those who accept the ways of the world and those who accept God's ways. Eventually, the spiritually reborn children of God will stick out like sore thumbs from the world's perspective and like bright beacons of light in an otherwise dark world from God's perspective. Inevitably, the world will seek to put these lights out but they shall not succeed.

God's chosen people, the Jews, have always anticipated the Christ would subdue their enemies, rid the world of evil, and rule justly and with authority from the throne of David forever and this shall indeed happen. However, God's purpose for man would not be served if, upon Jesus Christ's triumphant return, mankind would be damned to eternal separation from God because of their sins. The wages of the sins of the world had to be paid first. Mankind would then be able to not only reign with Christ but also become one with Him upon His triumphant return. The salvation of mankind had to be achieved before his liberation and unification with God. The gospel of Christ is the power of God unto salvation to every one that believes; to the Jew first and also to the Greek (Romans 1:16).

We have discussed in this chapter how our triune Godhead, through faith, created all things, and how each of His children has access to this limitless faith. In the next chapter, we shall discuss why man is the only created being to have access to this faith and why God created man in His image and after His likeness. Through the death and resurrection of His Son, Jesus the Christ, God has successfully restored unto Himself the called among mankind, and all things created during Creation week. His master plan is close to completion. Very soon mankind will become completely one with God through Jesus Christ, and all will be perfect as was originally intended. All that is left to be accomplished is for every person who is called by God to have an opportunity to accept God's free offer of redemption.

However, God allotted a certain amount of time to execute His master plan. Once that time has elapsed, God's offer of salvation will be taken off the proverbial table.

Now the question is, are you saved in and through Christ? Have you, by faith, accepted His free offer of pardon and of salvation? Is your faith a living and vital faith, or is it a vain and baseless faith? After all, it does make a difference. Your answers to these questions have eternal consequences, and time is running out.

Chapter Two

The Creation of Man In God's Image After Their Likeness

In this chapter we shall take a closer look at what it means to be made in the image and after the likeness of God and its implications for us as believers in Christ. Every human being was created to look like and have the characteristics of God so that we may be compatible enough with Him that He can abide in us and we in Him as one. We must be holy because He is Holy. Our sins have made us incompatible for this purpose, but our redemption in Christ has allowed us to be transformed into the image and likeness of Jesus, Who is the express image of God. Thus we are restored to our originally created state.

The Creation of Man

Genesis 1:26-27 tell us that, on the sixth day of creation week, God said:

> Let us make man in our image, after our likeness.
> . . . So God created man in his own image, in the

image of God created he him; male and female
created he them.

The Hebrew word for "image" is *tselem*, which
means "resemblance." The Hebrew word for "likeness"
is *demuwth*, which means "manner or similitude."
Therefore man was made to resemble the appearance
and to have attributes similar to those of God. Adam and
Eve and their progeny were truly created to mirror God
in every way. It is, therefore, appropriate to conclude
that, before their fall, Adam and Eve were the physical
manifestations of God on earth. Being one with God,
albeit through innocence rather than glory, their pre-Fall
relationship with God was so close that it must have
been extremely debilitating for Adam and Eve to grasp
what they had lost as a result of their sin of
disobedience.

God formed us of the dust of the ground and
breathed into our nostrils the breath of life (Genesis
2:7). As a result, every breath we take should be a
testament to us that God exists; that we live because He
gave us the breath of life (Acts 17: 25) and that we were
created to have His life in us. We thereby became souls
which are alive through and by the breath of God and
capable of living in the physical realm.

According to Genesis 1:26-28 and Genesis 2:7, the
creation of the soul and body of Adam occurred at the
same time. Since he was created in the image and after
the likeness of God, then both his soul and body
resembled God in appearance and manner. Adam was
also given a mind of his own so that he, by his own
volition, could be fully persuaded to obey or to disobey
God (Romans 14:5).

Thus, each of us was created to have a body, a soul

and a mind. This is exactly the makeup of our triune Godhead. Jesus Christ is head of the Body of God; and we, the children of God, comprise the Body of Christ (Romans 12:5; 1 Corinthians 12:12-14). There are passages too numerous to cite that establish the Holy Spirit is the Spirit of God (e.g., Matthew 28:19; John 14:26) in Whom the children of God live (Galatians 5:25). Leviticus 24:12, Romans 8:27; 11:34, and 1 Corinthians 2:16 all talk about the mind of God the Father, God the Son, and God the Holy Spirit. Man was created to be "filled with all the fullness of God" (Ephesians 3:19)—body, soul, and mind.

Man's Endowment with the Appearance and Characteristics of God

With respect to our being created in the image of God (Genesis 5:1-2; 9:6), what do the Holy Scriptures tell us about what God looks like? John 4:24 tells us that God is a Spirit. Ezekiel 1:26-28 provides a limited description of the appearance of God:

> And above the firmament that was over their heads was the likeness of a throne, as the appearance of a sapphire stone: and upon the likeness of the throne was the likeness as the appearance of a man above upon it.
>
> And I saw as the colour of amber, as the appearance of fire round about within it, from the appearance of his loins even upward, and from the appearance of his loins even downward, I saw as it were the appearance of fire, and it had brightness round about.
>
> As the appearance of the bow that is in the cloud in the day of rain, so was the appearance of the brightness round about. This was the

> appearance of the likeness of the glory of the
> LORD. And when I saw it, I fell upon my face, and
> I heard a voice of one that spoke.

According to these verses, God has the appearance of a man with the loins of a man. Nothing else is said about the appearance of God. Instead, these passages provide us with a vivid description of the glory of God, the likes of which we have yet to attain. From the waist up, God's glory looked like the color of amber that appeared to have fire around and within it. The glory surrounding His lower body had the appearance of fire, but with a brightness around it (Ezekiel 8:2). The throne of God had a rainbow around it (Revelation 4:2-3). According to 2 Corinthians 3:18, every one of God's children, once glorified, will have the same glory as the Lord.

> But we all, with open face beholding as in a glass
> the glory of the Lord, are changed into the same
> image from glory to glory, even as by the Spirit of
> the Lord.

We therefore were made, both physically and spiritually, in our triune God's image, but Their glory was withheld from Adam and Eve pending their passing God's test of obedience.

Equally important as being made to look like God is the fact that we were also made to have the characteristics and mannerisms of God. Since God, Jesus, and the Holy Spirit are one, the attributes of any one of Them are the attributes of all of Them. The more our oneness with Them is perfected, the more Their attributes become our attributes.

With respect to the attributes of God the Father, the Holy Scriptures tell us that God is perfect (Matthew 5:48). God the Father cannot lie (Numbers 23:19; Titus 1:1-2; Hebrews 6:18). He is truth, is without iniquity, just and right (Deuteronomy 32:4; Psalm 31:5). He is holy (Leviticus 11:44-45; 1 Peter 1:15-16), light (1 John 1:5), almighty (Genesis 17:1) and the great I AM (Exodus 3:14). He is love (1 John 4:8,16), and He is faithful (Deuteronomy 7:9; 1 Corinthians 1:9; 1 Thessalonians 5:24).

We therefore were created to be perfect, truthful, holy, love and faithful. We were also created to be light in which nothing dark or evil can dwell. We were created, not only to experience love, but to have uncompromising, unconditional, pure love as a part of our very nature. We were created have the heart of God and to be full of faith. Thus, it is our creative function to share in the experience of being God. We shall participate with God in the performance of whatever is in His mind to do.

Jesus, being the literal Word of God, can be nothing but consistent with the Almighty God. When God speaks, Jesus is the words that are spoken. God, therefore, speaks living words consisting of Himself.

In Psalm 12:6, it is written:

> The words of the LORD are pure words: as silver
> tried in a furnace of earth, purified seven times.

Hebrews 4:12-13 describe the Word of God as being alive, powerful, sharp enough to divide asunder soul and spirit and joint and marrow, able to discern the thoughts and intents of the heart, and able to see all things hidden and open. John 14:6 says that Jesus, the Son of God, is the Way, the Truth, and the Life. Hebrews 7:26 tells us more about the attributes of Jesus, the Son of God. It describes Jesus as "holy, harmless, undefiled, separate from sinners, and made higher than the heavens." A wonderful description of the characteristics of Jesus and, consequently, every child of God, is given by Jesus Himself in what is commonly referred to as the Beatitudes (Matthew 5:1-12). These verses describe the Godly characteristics of the children of God, who are conformed to His image (Romans 8:29). John 1:4 describes Jesus as being the life which is the light of men. It is this very life force that will sustain us throughout eternity as members of the Body of Christ. All that Jesus is, we were created to be.

There are numerous Scriptural references that describe the attributes of the Spirit of God, who is also referred to as the Holy Ghost. The Holy Ghost is described as the seven Spirits of God that have been sent forth into all the earth (Revelation 4:5; 5:6). In Isaiah 11:1-2, God defines the sevenfold Spirit of God as being the Spirit of the Lord, the Spirit of Wisdom, the Spirit of Understanding, the Spirit of Counsel, the Spirit of Might, the Spirit of Knowledge and the Spirit of the Fear of the Lord. Since we were created to be one with the Holy Spirit, we were made to have the sevenfold Spirit of God dwell in us and we in Him.

First John 5:6 tells us that it is the Spirit that bears witness to all things because He is the Spirit of truth. Other scriptural passages describe the Holy Ghost as the Spirit of Faith (2 Corinthians 4:13), the Spirit of Adoption (Romans 8:15), the Spirit of Grace (Hebrews 10:29), and the Spirit of Glory (1 Peter 4:14). All of these are characteristics of the Holy Ghost in whose likeness all of mankind were created.

Galatians 5:22 tells us that the fruit of the Spirit is love, joy, peace, long-suffering, gentleness, goodness, faith, meekness and temperance. All of the attributes of the Spirit of God can be ascribed to Jesus and to God the Father. Jesus' entire earthly experience was a constant exhibition of these fruits of the Spirit. Similarly, every child of God was created to bear the same fruit, having as we do the same characteristics as that of the Holy Spirit.

As the possessors of the characteristics, mannerisms and attributes of God the Father, God the Son, and God the Holy Ghost, Adam and Eve were the greatest among all creation. However, they lost these Godly characteristics upon their fall, but will possess them again upon their resurrection and ultimate glorification. These attributes currently exist in every spiritually reborn child of God and they will become the whole of our nature upon the perfection of our faith when we are similarly glorified in Christ Jesus.

Set forth below are but a sample of the passages in the Holy Scriptures which establish that, even in our yet to be glorified states, the spiritually reborn children of God can presently exhibit the characteristics of our triune God:

> With all lowliness and meekness, with long-suffering, forbearing one another in love. (Ephesians 4:2)
> Strengthened with all might, according to his glorious power, unto all patience and long-suffering with joyfulness. (Colossians 1:11)
> Put on therefore, as the elect of God, holy and

> beloved, bowels of mercies, kindness, humbleness
> of mind, meekness, long-suffering. (Colossians
> 3:12)
>   But thou, O man of God, flee these things;
> and follow after righteousness, godliness, faith,
> love, patience, meekness. (1 Timothy 6:11)

One of the Godly attributes that Adam and Eve were
not endowed with was the ability to discern the thoughts
and intents of the heart; that is, they were not
omniscient. Instead, they were given innocence. Had
Adam and Eve been omniscient, they surely would have
seen through Satan's deception. It was their desire to
become wise, with its attendant ability to discern
between good and evil, that caused them to disobey
God.

If Adam and Eve, through obedience, had eaten from
the Tree of Life instead of from the Tree of the
Knowledge of Good and Evil, they would have
immediately received immortal, glorified bodies and
would have secured their eternal status as the greatest of
God's creations. The millions and, indeed, billions of
offspring of a glorified Adam and Eve (Genesis 1:28)
would be the glorified children of God (1 John 3:1).
Because of their sin of disobedience, we who have
accepted God's redemption unto salvation, are the
physical temples of God yet to be glorified. We possess
all of the spiritual and physical characteristics of our
triune God but our ability to exhibit these qualities is yet
to be perfected.

The Purpose for Man's Creation
Every created thing, with the exception of man, was
created to exist as an entity separate from God, yet

under His authority. They reap the benefits of being creatures of God and honor God through their very existence. Mankind, however, was created to be one with God; to be the physical temples in whom God would indwell and through whom God would manifest Himself and exercise His dominion and authority over all creation. Not only was God originally intended to dwell in us, we were also created to dwell in God.

It is difficult for us to comprehend this type of oneness with God that is described and prayed for by Jesus in John 17. This is because it is our nature to want to be in control of our lives and we consider it an intrusion for someone else to dictate how we live. We do not realize that our lives are already lost; destined for destruction and that only by allowing God's life to merge with ours can we eternally save our lives. We need not be afraid of God living in us and we in Him. He wants to be an active participant in our lives. He wants to be a part of every breath we take; every thought we have and every act we engage in. If we let Him in to this extent, He truly abides in us and we in Him.

Recently God gave me an excellent real-life illustration of what it means to let Him be an active participant in our lives. I was playing a round of golf with three friends; two were saved, and one was not. We were playing a competitive round of golf for bragging rights only. The object of golf is to put the ball in a hole several hundred yards away with the least amount of strokes. One of my tee shots landed directly behind a tree. I would have to take a penalty stroke to put the ball in play.

As I approached my ball and realized my dilemma, I

was immediately tempted to move my ball away from the tree and play it without taking the penalty stroke. I looked around and confirmed that none of my friends would know of my deception. I knew that God would know and that I risked immediate chastisement if I did this deceitful act. I fully expected to end up taking a penalty stroke one way or the other before this round of golf was over, but I reasoned to myself that maybe, just maybe, God would let this one slide.

Then God spoke to me and said, " If you deceitfully move that ball, you would be effectively keeping Me from playing with you. I caused you to hit the ball behind the tree for any of a number of reasons. I may want you to lose today so that I may be glorified through the way you handle the loss. I may want you to win today, but not at any cost. Your victory would be only as I have laid it out for you. Yet, further still, I may be actively playing the round of golf with your two saved friends as I am with you; win or lose. Finally, I may be using this entire golf outing to reach out to your unsaved friend. Indeed, I may be doing all of these things and more. In order for Me to do so, you must relinquish control and let Me live through you. Now that My Spirit is merged with your spirit, everything that happens in your life is orchestrated by Me, and it is not for you to disrupt my work with your selfish agendas."

I am happy to say I did not move my ball from behind the tree. I took a penalty stroke and proceeded with the round of golf, but the game took on added significance. Whether I win or lose in golf, or any other endeavor in life, the outcome is only important to me as it relates to the will of God. I now realize that God is an active participant during every second of my life, to the furtherance of His good work. The extent of my spiritual maturation determines the degree to which I am able to be used by God. He truly abides in me, and I in Him.

Just as every living creature gives glory and honor to God by being what they were created to be, we also give Him glory and honor by being what we were created to be. However, He will not force Himself upon us. We have to willingly honor Him by giving ourselves over to Him. In return we become one with Him and will forever abide in God and He in us, in answer to the high priestly prayer of our Lord and Savior Jesus Christ (John 17).

In preparation for this holy union with God, mankind was created to be compatible with God by possessing the attributes and characteristics of God. Up until mankind's fall, there was no way to distinguish between the attributes and characteristics of God and those of Adam and Eve. Adam and Eve communed with God in a way that allowed them to exercise all of the power, dominion and authority of God. They were the most powerful beings created by God, and they ruled the world with their God-given authority. It is called the "fall of man" because Adam and Eve enjoyed a far higher state of existence before they sinned.

Mankind is the apex of all of God's creations. No other creature has a more important role in God's master plan. Thus, mankind was the last to be created. We were created to be the holy, physical temples of God in and through whom God would exercise His dominion over all creation. Because of this glorious function, unlike any other created thing, we were created in the image and after the likeness of our Creator. It is our intended function that defines our significance and thus our place in the creative order of things. Absent this utility, we would be just like every other created thing, in our own image and after our own likeness. As a result of the fall of Adam and Eve, this holy privilege is now destined for those of us chosen and called according to God's purpose. God becomes spiritually one with every child of His at the moment of their spiritual rebirths. That oneness becomes complete upon our glorification when Christ returns. We will be inseparable from God to the same extent that Jesus is inseparable from God.

What it actually means to be a child of God is almost too incredible to comprehend. God is all-knowing, all-powerful and all-present. Because we were made in God's image and after His likeness, we were created to also be all-knowing, all-powerful and all-present, and yet not us, but God who lives in and through us. We possess these awesome qualities only because God does. We must encourage each other unabashedly with this message and spread the good news to those who are lost.

The fact that we were created to possess the mannerisms, characteristics and attributes of God is a clear indication that our creative purpose requires us to be mirror images of God. The revelation of that creative purpose is unequivocally set forth with precise bluntness by Jesus Himself as recorded in the Gospel of John.

In John 17, Jesus interceded on behalf of the chosen people of God and prayed that they would become one with God just like Jesus is one with Him. In order for us to become one with God to the same extent that Jesus is one with Him, we have to choose God's way over our own way. We have to give up our individual existence independent from God, because the only existence separate from God is death. We are required to lose our lives and all the benefits thereof so that we can regain them, and yet not our lives, but God's life.

Specifically, John 17:11, 21-23 tell us that Jesus prayed that we may become one with God as He is one with Him. The significance of John 17, in its entirety, and specifically these four verses, in terms of understanding what God intended us to be when He made us in His image and after His likeness, cannot be overstated. It is important enough that we should look at the issue of oneness set forth in these four verses as translated in the New Living Translation (NLT); the New King James Version (NKJV) and the New American Standard Bible (NASB).

John 17:11 NLT   Holy Father, keep them and care for them—all those you have given me—so that they will be united just as we are.

NKJV   Holy Father, keep through Your name those whom You have given Me, that they may be one as We are.

NASB   Holy Father, keep them in Your name, the name which You have given Me, that they may be one even as We are.

John 17:21 NLT   My prayer for all of them is that they will be one, just as you and I are one, Father—that just as you are in me and I am in you, so they will be in us.

	NKJV	[T]hat they all may be one, as You, Father, are in Me, and I in You; that they also may be in Us.
	NASB	[T]hat they may all be one; even as You, Father, are in Me and I in You, that they also may be in Us.
John 17:22	NLT	I have given them the glory you gave me, so that they may be one, as we are.
	NKJV	And the glory which You gave Me I have given them, that they may be one just as We are one.
	NASB	The glory which You have given Me I have given to them, that they may be one, just as We are one.
John 17:23	NLT	I in them and you in me, all being perfected into one.
	NKJV	I in them, and You in Me; that they may be made perfect in one.
	NASB	I in them and You in Me, that they may be perfected in unity.

In John 17:11, our Lord and Savior prays that God will keep out of the world all of us who are called "in His name." We know that God the Father, God the Son, and God the Holy Ghost all carry the same name (Matthew 28:19). So one interpretation of this phrase would be that when we abide *in* Jesus and Jesus abides *in* us, we are, literally, "*in* His name." We are kept in our triune Godhead until our glorification, when we become one with our God to the same extent that Jesus and God the Father are one.

If I were to keep a child and raise him in my name, I in essence would be adopting him, and he would have my name. He would be an heir to all of my possessions and would share in the daily responsibilities of managing the family's affairs. When this verse is viewed in the context of the other three verses, we have some measure of appreciation as to what Jesus may have meant by asking God to keep us in the name of our triune Godhead. When our God abides in us and we in Him, we are adopted by Him. As a consequence, we take on His name and all of the benefits and responsibilities associated therewith. Galatians 4:4-7 states:

> But when the fullness of the time was come, God sent forth his Son, made of a woman, made under the law, To redeem them that were under the law, that we might receive the adoption of sons. And because ye are sons, God hath sent forth the Spirit of his Son into your hearts, crying, Abba, Father. Wherefore thou art no more a servant, but a son; and if a son, then an heir of God through Christ.

The Greek word *huiothesia* is used for the phrase "adoption of sons." It means sonship conferred as opposed to sonship by birth. Jesus is the only Son of God by birth. Through our faith in Jesus Christ, we are adopted as sons of God; the Spirit of Jesus lives in our hearts and we are heirs of God through Christ (Ephesians 1:3-12).

We are not only adopted by God and given all of the

privileges, rights and responsibilities attendant to one who carries His name, but we also literally live in His name and He lives in us. Thus, when we ask anything, while in this state of mutual inhabitation "in His name," He will do it (John 14:14; 16:23). We have to abide in our triune God and He in us in order for us to be in a position to have our prayers answered. So many of us end our prayers to God with the perfunctory "In the name of Jesus Christ, our Lord and Savior" without appreciating that it is our spiritual relationship with God that determines whether we are "in His name." Our prayers are answered because God abides in us and we in Him, not because we rotely call upon His name at the end of every prayer. It is only then that we are truly "in His name." This mutual indwelling between the children of God and their Father will result in a unification with God that mirrors the oneness Jesus has with His Father.

Verse 21 defines that unification the children of God will experience when they become one with their Father. Just as God is in Jesus and Jesus is in God, so will we be in Them. In other words, we will all be in each other. This oneness does not come about solely as a result of souls joining with God individually. It comes about when all reborn souls join with one another and with God collectively, much like a marriage (Ephesians 5:30-32).

This type of oneness is inseparable, and the component parts are indistinguishable. Oneness to this extent gives God full and complete control to be all that He is through us, individually and collectively. Jesus tells us in John 14:10 that the two-way habitation between Him and the Father does not allow Him to speak on His own authority. It allows God the Father,

Who dwells in Jesus, to speak on His own authority through Jesus. When we become one with God to this extent, we will not do anything on our own authority. God, Who will be indwelling us, will be doing everything through us on His own authority.

Verse 22 of John 17 describes how this oneness will be effectuated. Jesus gives us the same glory that God gave Him. Jesus demonstrated the glory God gave Him at the transfiguration (Luke 9:28-30). We are being transformed daily into this same glory by the Holy Spirit (2 Corinthians 3:18). It is this transformation that enables us to become completely one with our triune Godhead.

Verse 23 further explains that, as we become more and more in Them and They in us, Their glory becomes more and more our glory as we are perfected into one. As members of the Body of Christ, we are in Jesus and He is in us. Since Jesus and God are one, we are also in God and God is in us. It is only through this type of indivisible unity that we can look and act like God. It is only through this form of oneness that we can truly say that we are in the image and after the likeness of our triune Godhead.

Since Jesus is described as the faithful witness in Revelation 1:5, the faithfulness of His prayer will cause it to be answered. Jesus never made a petition to God, His Father, that was not realized. After all, He is Himself God. The first scriptural indication that Jesus' faithful prayer in John 17 was being realized was the day of Pentecost when those gathered "were all with one accord in one place" (Acts 2:1). Upon each of them receiving the Holy Spirit, they knew that Jesus is in the Father; that the Father is in Jesus; that they are in Jesus;

that Jesus is in them; that they are in God; and that God is in them (John 14:20). They knew that they were all one with their triune Godhead. They immediately demonstrated the awesome power attendant to their oneness with God by spreading the gospel of Jesus Christ, speaking languages never before spoken by them.

When we become one with God, He will demonstrate the same power and control through us as He did through Jesus and His disciples. As previously stated, Adam was a prototype of Jesus, but without the glory of God and without the ability to tell the difference between good and evil. Adam never attained that level of perfection because of his sin. However, the death and resurrection of Jesus will allow for Adam and his chosen descendants, whose names are written in the Book of Life, to receive their incorruptible bodies, the glory of God, and the ability to discern between good and evil, thereby making us, through loving obedience, one with God and friends of Jesus (John 15:10-15). This type of friendship is closer than any imaginable.

During these last days of the so-called "church age," the elect of God are beginning to comprehend the power attendant to being individually and collectively one with God through Jesus the Christ and, at the same time, one with each other. The more we experience this degree of oneness with God, the more empowered we become, just as the saints at the Pentecost were empowered. At that time, the Holy Spirit was sent into the world to indwell the elect of God. He will continue to indwell every person who is spiritually reborn until our glorified perfection.

Can any of us truly say that we fully comprehend the

significance of being created to be one with God? This wonderful eventuality has not been the topic of many sermons. Nor has it been the prolific subject of biblical literature. However, its absence from the lips and pages of professing Christians does not detract from the reality of its truth. Indeed, it is this fundamental truth that answers the questions of why our obedience to God was tested in the Garden of Eden; why Satan continually seeks to destroy us and why God has chosen to redeem us. Upon our perfection, we shall approach the very throne of God and gaze into His eyes and prayerfully say "Oh, Father God, with all of my substance I give You thanks and praise because You are, I am, and we are one."

If this does not cause you to spiritually, if not physically, jump out of your seat and do a victory dance, then you have yet to be spiritually reborn. Should this be the case with you, I pray that you take this opportunity to accept the death and resurrection of Jesus Christ for the forgiveness of your sins, and be born as a child of God. Eternal salvation and oneness with God is available to any "one" who seeks to be all that he or she was created to be.

CHAPTER THREE

THE FALL OF MAN

The overriding lesson to be gleaned from the Holy Scriptures is that love of God can only be demonstrated through obedience to God. God is 100 percent true, pure, uncompromising and unconditional love. Love is as much a part of God as we are human. Love is who and what God is. As previously stated, we have to be compatible with God in every way in order to become one with Him. Therefore it is essential that we possess this Godly characteristic. Before perfecting His oneness with Adam and Eve, God wanted to determine whether they would demonstrate this degree of love for Him by placing obedience to Him above everything else, including their own desires.

This chapter focuses on God's obedience test of Adam and Eve from the perspective of the angelic hosts who witnessed it. We discuss how Satan's sin of pride caused him to become a deceptive player in this test. We examine why Adam and Eve's failure of God's obedience test demonstrated their complete lack of love for their Creator and the catastrophic consequences of their disobedience to God.

Praise be to God for not letting the story of mankind end with their sin of disobedience. God promised to redeem both Adam and Eve and their progeny and demonstrated His eternal love for us all by having His only begotten Son deliver on that promise.

The Creation of the Angels

We know from the Word of God that the angels were created for the purpose of worshiping and praising God and being ministering servants. The hosts of heaven have no other function. We also know that the physical realm was created for the sole purpose of providing a physical means through which God may demonstrate His awesome power, magnificent perfection and limitless grace.

All things created exist and consist by and through God and they honor and glorify Him by the perfect order of their ways. Every living creature was made in its own image and after its own kind, except for man, who was created in the image and after the likeness of God. There is no greater way to honor and glorify God than to be what we were created to be. This is no less true for the angels.

The Word of God tells us something about these spiritual beings called angels, who were created to live in the timeless existence with God that we call eternity and whom the apostle Paul cautions us not to worship (Colossians 2:18). One order of these angelic beings are the cherubim. The word "cherubim" is plural and is derived from the Hebrew word *kărūbh*. According to Ezekiel 1:5-25 and 10:13-22, each of these beings has four faces and four wings, with the hands of a man under their wings. They have the faces of a man, the most intelligent creature created; of a lion, the greatest animal of prey; of an ox, the strongest beast of burden; and of an eagle, the king of the air. The cherubim apparently possess intelligence, ferocity, strength and regality; characteristics often symbolized by these four creatures. The soles of their feet are described as being like the soles of calves' feet and these beings sparkle like the color of burnished brass. They come and go like flashes of lightning. They are obviously formidable and splendid creations. Yet, with all of their power and splendor, they were not created in the image or after the likeness of God.

The Holy Scriptures describe yet another form of heavenly being that appears to be related to and inseparable from the cherubim. They are sometimes referred to as the ophanin. The prophet Ezekiel describes them as having the appearance of a beryl stone. Each one of these magnificent creatures looked the same—a wheel in the middle of a wheel. They each had eyes all over their bodies. Each of the ophanin was paired with a cherub. Whatever and wherever the cherub did or went, so did and so went the wheels, because the spirit of the cherub was in the ophanin (Ezekiel 1:15-21, 10:9-17). Despite the wonder and purpose of these spiritual beings, they also were not created in the image or after the likeness of God.

Isaiah 6:2-3 describes a third form of angelic being created by God: the seraphim. Each of these beings has six wings; two cover their faces, two their feet, and with two they fly. The word "seraphim" was taken from the Hebrew word *sārāph,* which means "burners or burning ones." Despite the unique beauty and majesty of these angelic beings, they were not made in the image or after the likeness of God.

All of these angelic creatures were made to be ministering servants (Psalm 104:4; Hebrews 1:14). Though mighty, they were sometimes charged with error (Job 4:18) and considered unclean in the sight of God (Job 15:15). Thus the angels are capable of sinning before God. Yet, as we shall see, they were nonetheless allowed by God to perform a ministerial service. Angels are referred to as the sons of God (Job 1:6; 2:1). Being spirits, they therefore must be spiritual sons of God. Though asexual (Matthew 22:30), they are always referred to in the masculine sense. They are to be distinguished from mankind in that mankind is both male and female and is destined to be the physical and spiritual children of God. Scripture tells us that thousands upon thousands of angels were created (Revelation 5:11). In fact, they are innumerable (Hebrews 12:22). If Jesus had but asked, His Father would have given Him more than twelve legions of angels (Matthew 26:53).

The scriptural descriptions of angels suggest that there are categories of angels and that certain angels may have specialized functions. There is Michael the Archangel (Jude 9), the highest in the order of the angels, who leads God's angels into combat (Daniel 10:13, 21; 12:1; Revelation 12:7). There are angelic messengers such as Gabriel, who deliver messages from God (Daniel 8:16; Luke 1:19, 26).

The cherubim are apparently guardian and covering angels; they were responsible for keeping Adam and Eve out of the Garden of Eden after their expulsion (Genesis 3:24). The cherubim covered the mercy seat of

God (Exodus 25:18-20) and are constantly in the presence of the Glory of God (Ezekiel 10:1-22). The cherubim are often associated with covering God's judgment. This may partially explain why Satan, a fallen cherub (Ezekiel 28:14), accuses us daily before the throne of God, requesting that God render unto us the judgment we so rightly deserve (Revelation 12:10) instead of seeking to cover our judgment as he was created to do.

The seraphim continually fly in the presence of God declaring His Holiness, praising and worshiping Him (Isaiah 6:1-3). They are associated with sacrificing and cleansing (Isaiah 6:5-7).

According to Hebrews 1:13-14, none of the angels created by God will sit at His right hand and neither will He make their enemies their footstool. This He gives only to Jesus. Those same verses do tell us, however, that all angels are ministering spirits sent forth to minister, not just to God, but also to all of us who shall be heirs of salvation.

Satan's Rebellion Against God

Of course the most infamous angelic being who witnessed creation week was Lucifer, who, before he sinned against God from the beginning (1 John 3:8), was described in Ezekiel 28:14 as "the anointed cherub." Being a cherub, Lucifer (later known as Satan) was also created to have four faces; one of a man; one of a lion, one of an ox and one of an eagle. He is therefore intelligent, ferocious, powerful and regal. As all other cherubim, he has four wings, with the hands of a man under his wings. The soles of his feet are like calves' feet that sparkle like burnished brass, and he

goes and comes as a flash of lightning. Satan would also
have an ophanin, who possesses his spirit, by his side
wherever he goes. Very seldom will you see Satan
depicted as he truly is.

It is of some significance that Satan was created to
be a covering cherub (Ezekiel 28:14, 16). As previously
stated, two cherubim covered the mercy seat with their
wings (Exodus 25:18-20). The Hebrew words from
which we get the phrase "mercy seat" have been
translated to mean "place or object of covering,
concealment, redemption, ransom and atonement." This
place of covering (i.e., "mercy seat") was where the
Jewish high priest would sprinkle the blood of sacrificed
animals for the forgiveness of the sins of the nation.
Apparently, one of the creative functions of the
cherubim was to cover this place of atonement where
God sometimes dwelt (Psalm 80:1). Upon the ultimate
sacrifice of Jesus, there is no longer any need for the
continuing covering of the sins of the world because
they were forever forgiven by the death and resurrection
of Jesus Christ. Because of his sin of pride, Satan lost
his desire to cover. Now he not only seeks the execution
of God's judgments upon mankind but also consistently
seeks to persuade mankind to reject the sacrificial death
of Jesus Christ on their behalf.

Satan is one of the most astounding spiritual beings
created by God and, like all cherubim, has always been
associated with the judgment of God. According to
Ezekiel 28, Satan was present in the Garden of Eden and
had every precious stone as his covering, which
included the sardius, topaz, diamond, beryl, onyx,
jasper, sapphire, emerald, carbuncle and gold.

It is of interest to note that every one of the precious

stones that covered Lucifer were required to be included in the four rows of stones set in gold in the breastplate of judgment worn by Aaron, the first Jewish high priest (Exodus 28:15-21). Also included in the breastplate were jacinth, agate and amethyst. Aaron and his seed were to continually bear the judgment of Israel upon their hearts by wearing this breastplate whenever they came before the Lord. Perhaps this was done as a constant testimony to God that man's continual state of sin, and consequently any judgment thereof, must be rendered in the context of the deception of one of His highest covering cherubim.

Many of these precious stones appear in the Holy Scriptures as adornments to the foundations of the new Jerusalem, which shall be made of pure gold and shall be the habitation of all whose names are written in the Lamb's Book of Life (Revelation 21:9-27). God, in His eternal wisdom, uses the same types of precious stones—which initially covered Lucifer, before he became Satan, and which covered the breastplate of judgment worn by the high priest of the twelve tribes of Israel until their redemption through Jesus Christ—to cover the twelve foundations of the Holy City that will house the people of God. Because God is perfect in all His ways, His use of these stones in these ways has a significance which shall one day be fully revealed to us.

We have already discussed how Ezekiel 28:11-19 describe the beauty and magnificence of Satan before his fall. Ezekiel 28:13 indicates that, before his sin of pride, Satan possessed wonderful timbrels and pipes with which he provided tremendous musical worship of God. According to verses 14 and 16, he had access to the holy mountain of God and walked up and down in the midst of the stones of fire. Yet even Satan was never made in the image and after the likeness of God.

It appears from these same passages that, given his awesome power and splendor (Ezekiel 28:17), Satan was unable to remain a ministering servant who sought to cover God's judgment of mankind. Isaiah 14:12-33 vividly describe the fall of Satan when iniquity was found in him. According to these verses, Satan was sinless before God at some point during his existence. First John 3:8 tells us that the devil sinned from the beginning; that is, Satan first sinned "in the beginning," not before the beginning. John 8:44 tells us that Satan was a murderer from the beginning. Something happened either before, during or immediately after creation week that caused pride to swell up in his heart and caused Satan to rebel against God and seek to usurp, through deception, God's plan for mankind by murdering us through the commission of sin. Satan's tremendous self-pride prevented him from accepting his creative covering purpose in God's master plan.

The Holy Scriptures reveal that, just like Adam and Eve, Satan did not know good or evil before he sinned. His sin of pride was the source of his knowledge of evil, which he clearly possessed by the time he tempted Eve. There is no indication in the Holy Word of God that Satan ever came to know good. He possesses only an evil nature. There is no truth in him (John 8:44). Satan can therefore do only what he knows how to do, and that is evil. To know evil necessitates the commission of sin. Just like a man biblically knows a woman when he has sexual intercourse with her, one cannot know sin unless he engages in it. When Satan sinned against God, he became one with sin, taking on a sin nature.

There is no greater deceiver or liar than Satan, for it is written that he is the "father of lies" (John 8:44) and could appear as an angel of light (2 Corinthians 11:13-14). As a result of his deception of Adam and Eve, Satan was cursed. God prophesied that Satan would ultimately be destroyed by Jesus Christ, the seed of the woman (Genesis 3:14-15). Satan will be bound for 1,000 years, loosed for a while, and then eternally removed from the presence of God, God's children, and all creation (Revelation 20:1-15).

Satan purposed to overcome this curse by causing Jesus to sin and thereby bring into condemnation the souls of a sinful mankind. For Adam and Eve, their sin was in disobeying God and obeying Satan. Their obedience to Satan caused them, and their offspring, to take on Satan's sin nature and to become one with him as his children. Thus, it is written of those who choose Satan over God:

> Ye are of your father the devil, and the lusts of your father ye will do. He was a murderer from the beginning, and abode not in the truth, because there is no truth in him. When he speaketh a lie, he speaketh of his own: for he is a liar, and the father of it. (John 8:44)

Because Adam and Eve ate from the Tree of the Knowledge of Good and Evil, they also knew good. Anyone with free will who possesses such dual knowledge, through sin, cannot coexist with God because, invariably, evil will be chosen; despite having the knowledge of good. Once sin is chosen, we can no longer be one with God because a person cannot be one with both Satan and God. Death, which is the complete physical and spiritual separation from God, is the penalty for sin. Just like Adam and Eve, Satan understood all too well the wages of his sin. He nonetheless believed that he could avoid that fate if he could become one with mankind, through sin, and use us to assist him in his rebellion against God.

Satan lost his desire to serve God as a covering cherub when iniquity was found in his heart, but he continues to have access to the throne of God. For instance, in Job 1:6-7, well after the creation of all things, Satan presented himself before God along with the other angelic sons of God to discuss his goings and comings and God's servant Job. God often uses His enemies to effectuate His will. He did so with the heathen kings during the postexilic era of the Israelites. God permits Satan to continually test His highest creation to determine our love of God or our love of self.

Psalm 33:6 tells us that God spoke all of creation, including the angels, into existence. According to Genesis 2:1-2, God rested on the seventh day of creation, having completed the creation of the heavens and the earth. Nehemiah 9:6 provides some guidance as to the order of that creative process:

> Thou, even thou, art LORD alone; thou hast made heaven, the heaven of heavens, with all their host, the earth, and all things that are therein, the seas, and all that is therein, and thou preservest them all; and the host of heaven worshipeth thee.

This verse confirms that God created the celestial heavens, His spiritual kingdom, the earth and all that is in it. With respect to the earth, God created the planet, formed the lands and seas, created its animal inhabitants, and created man to exercise dominion over all the earth. After God created man, He rested, further implying that the entire creative process had been completed. Clearly, the creation of the spiritual realm occurred prior to the creation of man.

Since God's spiritual kingdom and its angelic citizens were created before He created the physical realm (Genesis 1:1; Nehemiah 9:6; Job 38:4-7; Psalm 104:4-5), the angels, who reside in His presence, witnessed every phase of the creation of the physical realm (Job 38:4-7). The angelic hosts were firsthand witnesses to the creation of the world and would have heard every verbal command of God. They would have seen His creative will supernaturally realized day by day as each command was uttered. As the order of things became revealed to them, they no doubt realized the fullness of God's creative design and their role in it. The angels would have also understood that the order in which all seen and unseen things were creatively realized spoke volumes about the ever-increasing significance and level of importance attributed to each ensuing phase of the creative process according to God's Holy will.

Just like all the other angels, Satan would have been present during creation week and would have observed the order of God's creative process. With access to the throne of God, he would have had a front row perspective of the awesome power, authority and faithfulness of God being demonstrated as each verbal creative command was effectuated by His Living Word, including the last and most important creative utterance of God: "Let us make man in our image, after our likeness."

Satan understood the significance of this statement and knew that man was purposed to mirror God in appearance and characteristics and be above all of God's creations, including the angels. He had to know that God intended to become one with man so that he could manifest Himself in and through man. One of the definitions given for the word "manifestation" in the *Webster's New World Dictionary* could not be more on point: "a form in which a being manifests itself or is thought to manifest itself, especially the material or bodily form of a spirit." Satan realized that his creative role, as well as that of the other angels, was to be that of ministering servants to God and eventually to every human being through whom God manifests Himself.

Satan was so proud of his beauty, splendor, and power that he thought himself greater than man and equal to God. It is apparent that he could not bring himself to serve either. According to Isaiah 14:14, Satan said in his heart that he will be *like* the Most High, not *greater than* the Most High. Even Satan recognized, in his moment of sin, that no creature can be greater than the Most High. Satan also knew that only man was made in the image and after the likeness of the Most High. We were given the privilege of being what Satan wanted to be. Satan was not content with his position in God's ordered creation, having angelic attributes after his own kind. Satan's pride prevented him from accepting the fact that another creation of God could become one with God, especially since Satan would have to be subservient to that other creation. Satan, therefore, purposed in his heart that, in order for him to be like the Most High, he had to become one with mankind before God could do so.

Satan correctly reasoned that, should Adam and Eve sin, they and their progeny would have to suffer death in the form of eternal separation from God. This would make all of mankind available for Satan to become one with them through sin. He wanted to be worshiped by all creation. Since all creation revolves around mankind, Satan reasoned that, once he became master of mankind through sin, he would consequentially be master of all creation. Satan has always sought to have what God has; nothing more, because there is nothing more, and nothing less.

Knowing all things, God was aware of Satan's rebellious plan before Adam and Eve's obedience test. Yet God decided not to address Satan's sin. Instead, He allowed Satan to become an active participant in the test of Adam and Eve's love of God through obedience. Apparently, God wanted Satan to perform his creative function as a ministering servant by assisting in the administration of God's obedience test of Adam and Eve despite his sin of pride. If this is true, then Satan had to be aware that his attempt to deceive Adam and Eve was done with God's permission. If Adam and Eve had obeyed God despite Satan's deception, mankind would have been perfected in God and Satan's damnation would have been swift, immediate and eternal. Should Adam and Eve give in to sin by eating from the forbidden Tree of the Knowledge of Good and Evil, Satan would then be permitted to prove to God that every one of their offspring, given the free will to do so, would invariably choose evil over good.

Satan sought to present to God irrefutable evidence that dominion, power and authority cannot be effectively exercised by God through a creature who does not place love of others above love of self. Satan contended that mankind would fail to reciprocate the degree of selfless love which God exhibits toward them.

Having determined within himself to challenge God's authority by seeking to raise himself above his created estate to a status equal to God, Satan welcomed this ministerial task and, indeed, may have requested it. He set about to cause Adam and Eve to sin against God just as he later set about to cause Job to curse God to His face. Satan knew that the wages of Adam and Eve's sin would cause them to die through eternal physical and spiritual separation from God. They would then no longer possess the characteristics and attributes of God. They would be in the image and after the likeness of themselves (Genesis 5:3), becoming one with Satan in sin. God would not be able to become one with Adam and Eve while they were in this sinful state.

If mankind could be turned into an enemy of God, Satan's rebellion against God would take place in the physical realm where he would have dominion and authority and the spiritual realm where he had the support of a number of the angels (2 Peter 2:4; Jude 6). He mistakenly believed that he would then have the advantage over God. In reality, however, while Satan may have initially thrown the proverbial wrench into God's creative process, in the end, all will be restored to its original perfection and every person who chooses God's way over Satan's way will be restored to his rightful place as God's greatest creation and will become one with God. With his service complete, Satan will then be tossed into the eternal lake of fire.

By bringing about the fall of Adam and Eve, Satan temporarily usurped their authority and dominion over the earth to do with as he pleases (Luke 4:5-7). When Satan succeeded in deceiving Adam and Eve, they became Satan's captive; being one with him through sin and forced to do his bidding (2 Timothy 2:26). Satan was then able to work his rebellion against God through Adam and Eve and all of their offspring (Ephesians 2:2). Adam and Eve and their descendants were originally intended to be inhabited by God. Instead, we are inhabited by Satan. Satan's misuse of us has caused us all to sin and will result in our physical and spiritual deaths unless we are freed from these death sentences by accepting, in faith, the sacrificial death of Jesus Christ in our stead.

Our sin natures will cause us to invariably sin. Any sin, whether great or small, significant or insignificant, requires the same physical and spiritual death penalty. That is why it is impossible for any offspring of Adam and Eve to enter the Kingdom of Heaven if they do not accept God's sacrifice for the propitiation of their sins. No amount of obedience or good works can offset the death penalty required for just one sin, let alone many. It is unfortunate that many people believe that they will not suffer eternal damnation and separation from God because, for the most part, they have led decent and upstanding lives. They cannot fathom the fact that, even if they committed the most insignificant sin only once over their entire lifetime, they would still be deserving of eternal death because that one sin would make it impossible for them to co-exist with a sinless, Holy God; let alone enjoy a mutual inhabitation with Him.

It is for this reason that we needed, and received, a Messiah, a Savior, Who delivered us from our death penalties by dying in our place, and Who will give us the victory over death.

During the tribulation period, Satan's service to God will end when he initiates a war against God in heaven. Michael and God's holy angels will prevail against Satan and his fallen angels. God will cast them out of heaven into the earth (Revelation 12:7-9). When Jesus said, in Luke 10:18, that he "beheld Satan as lightning fall from heaven," one must keep in mind that Satan is a cherub and therefore he moves as a flash of lightning. Also, as previously discussed, Jesus Christ, the literal Word of God, is God and is the Alpha and the Omega, as stated in Revelation 1:8, 11. Therefore, not being confined to this world's temporal existence, He can speak in past tense about seeing Satan being cast out of heaven even though, according to this world's time, it has not yet happened.

Shortly after his permanent ouster from heaven, Satan will continue his war against God on the Earth. Jesus will prevail against Satan's earthly forces as well (Revelation 19:19-21). Satan's judgment occurred when Jesus sacrificed His sinless life on the cross; was resurrected by God and ascended into heaven (John 12:31; 16:7-11). That judgment will be enforced when Jesus returns at the end of the tribulation period. At that time, all of the enemies of God will be placed under the feet of Christ (1 Corinthians 15:27; Hebrews 2:8). Since all of God's children compose the Body of Christ, Satan and his minions will be placed under our feet (Romans 16:20).

In the original Greek text, the word *kekritai* means "has been judged." Jesus' innocent death for sins He did not commit paid the price for all the sins of mankind (1 John 2:2) and resulted in Satan's judgment approximately 2,000 years ago. Satan initially succeeded in causing us to fall from grace and to come under his authority, but the great love of God was demonstrated by allowing His living Word, which is a part of Himself, to become one of us in and through the person of Jesus Christ and to suffer our death penalties in our stead. His death forever frees us from the clutches of Satan. We need only accept, in faith, this sacrifice on our behalf.

Satan's Deception of Man

With direct access to the very throne of God, Satan observed God in all His splendor and glory and had to know that any power and magnificence he possessed as an angel paled in comparison to that of God. Yet, he obviously was not awed into submission by God's glory and power because he determined to establish his own agenda when permitted to intervene into God's obedience test of man by attempting to deceive Adam and Eve into believing that they could obtain, through sin, what God had already intended to freely give them through obedience.

Satan's deception of Adam and Eve was actually comprised of several deceptions. He first of all deceived Adam and Eve into believing that, as they then existed, they would never be more than what they were. For had Adam and Eve known that they were made to be one with God, they may never have believed the serpent's lie that they had to eat of the forbidden fruit to be like God. They must have thought that they were made after their own kind just like every other created thing.

This first deception was crucial to Satan's plan for their submission to him through the sin of disobedience.

It formed the basis for Adam and Eve's desire to be more than what they believed they were. Once Adam and Eve believed the lie that they would never be more than they were, Satan succeeded in deceiving them into believing that God lied to them in order to keep them from being like Him. This second deception was made possible because of the success of the first deception. Adam and Eve were willing to believe that God would lie to them because of their desire to improve their status quo in God's ordered creation.

Adam and Eve's willingness to believe that God would lie to them strongly suggests that they were unaware that they were created in the image and after the likeness of God, thereby possessing Godly characteristics and mannerisms. Since God cannot lie (Titus 1:2), Adam and Eve, before their fall, also could not lie. Had they known that this personality trait was from and of God, they would have known that the serpent, not God, was the liar. They must have seen the similarities between their character and that of God, but there is no indication in the Scriptures that they were ever told that they mirrored the image and likeness of God in every way or that they were created to become one with God. In order for them to pass the obedience test, Adam and Eve would have to obey God for no other reason than because they loved Him more than they loved themselves. They were not given the option to obey God because of what they could gain as a reward. It was to be obedience out of love or no obedience at all. Adam and Eve, by their choice of disobedience, established that their love of self was greater than any love they had for God.

As a result of Adam and Eve's love of self, it was

easy for Satan to accomplish the third deception. He deceived Adam and Eve into believing that they could improve their status in God's ordered creation by disobeying Him. God told Adam and Eve that the only way for them to ever suffer death was to disobey His edict not to eat of the forbidden fruit. Nonetheless, they were deceived into believing that, by eating this fruit in disobedience to God, they would not only continue to live but would also know the difference between good and evil, knowledge reserved only unto God.

These three deceptions brought about the fall of mankind who was created to be one with God by the grace of God. Their fall from grace, through sin, resulted in Satan, the father of sin, becoming one with them and their progeny, all having a sin nature just like Satan. Their sin should have ensured their permanent separation from God through death, which is the result of sin. But God through His infinite mercy decided to spare them and their descendants from the death sentences they so rightly deserved.

We were created to be inseparable from God, to be one with God. Eternal separation from God would be the antithesis of God's plan for us. Therefore God initiated a plan for our salvation. This redemptive plan was effectuated by the death and resurrection of Jesus Christ for sins He did not commit. As a result, only those of mankind who would reject God's free offer of eternal salvation and succumb to the same deception as did Adam and Eve, by choosing their own way over God's way, would be eternally damned—just as Satan's decision to sin against God resulted in his own eternal damnation as well as that of all the angels who followed his lead.

In Matthew 3:12, the wicked among mankind is depicted as the chaff; the righteous is referred to as the wheat. Instead of immediately destroying Satan and his fallen angels, God uses them to continually identify the spiritual chaff among mankind so that, in the end, God need only separate the wheat from the chaff. He will execute His judgment upon the chaff and become one with the wheat.

God's Obedience Test

Upon their creation Adam and Eve had the appearance and characteristics of God, yet they did not possess the knowledge of God. Obviously, the degree of Adam and Eve's oneness with God, which they enjoyed prior to their fall from grace, was not perfected and indeed was unknown to them. The Holy Scriptures tell us that they could only achieve this knowledge through obedience whereby they would be allowed to eat from the Tree of Life. Their lack of such knowledge made Adam and Eve susceptible to Satan's deceptions. Their lust to fulfill their personal desires led to their willful disobedience of God and embracement of Satan's temptations.

The entire Garden of Eden experience was set up to determine whether they would obey God until they ate from the Tree of Life, or disobey God by eating from the Tree of the Knowledge of Good and Evil (Genesis 2:15-17). If Adam and Eve had passed this initial test, there would have been no need for any of their offspring to be tested. Unfortunately, because they did not, their descendants have been tested by God on numerous occasions over time. For instance, in Genesis 22:1-14 Abraham was tested when he was asked to offer up his son Isaac. In Deuteronomy 8:2,16, the Holy Scriptures tell us that the Israelites were tested in the wilderness to prove their commitment to the Lord. Job was tested in Job 1:7-12. In fact, the faith of every child of God is continually tested so that, when proven, we can obtain the crown of life (1 Peter 1:7). This was the same prize that awaited Adam and Eve had they passed their test.

The dictates of Adam and Eve's test required that they be created with bodies that were perfect but capable of corruption, depending on their performance on the test. They were created with free wills because the test required them to choose to be obedient out of love for God or to choose disobedience out of love of self. With multiple options, free will is a necessity. God wanted to know if Adam and Eve loved Him enough to place obedience to Him above any selfish desires. When they chose to satisfy their own desires instead of the desire of God, they demonstrated the extent of their hatred of God. Their sin caused them to fall from grace and to be deserving of both physical and spiritual death.

Only upon our glorification, when we shall know all things, shall we know how Adam and Eve would have responded to this test absent Satan's deception. Satan was unable to discern the thoughts and intents of the hearts of Adam and Eve, and so he was more than willing to take part in this test because otherwise his desire to become one with man through sin would have to rest on whether they would disobey God on their own. Satan must have also known that Adam and Eve similarly did not possess the ability to discern the thoughts and intents of the hearts of others. He had to know that they could not tell the difference between good and evil. He was therefore able to deceive them into believing that the obtainment of this attribute would make them that much closer to being like God, but only by eating of the forbidden tree in direct disobedience to God.

Genesis 3:1-13 tell us the story of man's failure of God's obedience test. In order to tempt Adam and Eve, Satan deceptively possessed a serpent. His possession of the serpent was not done outside of the knowledge of God. God knew of Satan's deceptive intentions and allowed him to proceed with his plan. After all, there can be no greater measure of Adam and Eve's love of God than to test their obedience through temptation.

According to Genesis 1:26, Adam and Eve were given dominion over all the earth, which included every creeping thing, including serpents. In order for Adam and Eve to effectively exercise their dominion over the world, they had to possess enough power and authority to ensure the submission of the earth and everything in it. In our current fallen state, it is difficult for us to fully comprehend the awesome power and authority wielded by Adam and Eve before their fall. Though they may not have known it, they possessed the attributes and characteristics of God and were a legitimate force to be reckoned with. They were quite capable of exercising the dominion given to them by God over the earth.

But we need not stretch our imaginations too far to envision these two spectacular beings. Jesus is the last Adam (1 Corinthians 15:45), who possesses all of the attributes, glory and knowledge of God. When we look at the power and authority exercised by Jesus during His earthly life, as set forth in the Holy Scriptures, we can get a glimpse of the power and authority Adam and Eve possessed before their fall, absent God's glory and knowledge. For instance, Jesus calmed the seas by command (Mark 4:35-41), walked on water (Matthew 14:22-33), withered a fig tree by a curse (Matthew 21:17-20), and commanded fish to seek the fishermen's nets (Luke 5:1-11).

When questioned by the band of men and officers from the chief priests and Pharisees as to whether He was Jesus of Nazareth, as set forth in John 18:1-6, Jesus answered and said, "I am he." These words spoken by Jesus threw the men backward and onto the ground. This passage clearly demonstrates that Jesus is the same I AM as is God the Father, Who identified Himself by that name when asked by Moses in Exodus 3:14. It also demonstrates the complete control Jesus has over His limitless power. Jesus did exactly what He wanted to do to His accusers and nothing more.

Adam and Eve were not all that Jesus was during His earthly life because Jesus, being God, also possesses the glory and knowledge of God. He can discern the thoughts and intents of the hearts of men. These are Godly qualities that Adam and Eve could only attain through obedience. Nonetheless, they most likely exercised significant power and authority over nature and the animal kingdom. Clearly, they were powerful creatures and more than capable of ruling the world. Nothing on earth would dare challenge Adam and Eve's God-given authority over them.

This may explain why Adam and Eve would choose to believe one of God's creations under their God-given power and authority instead of God. The Holy Scriptures tell us that, of all the creatures under their dominion, the serpent was the most subtle (Genesis 3:1). In the books of Proverbs, Job and Matthew, the word "subtle" has been used to mean prudent on the one hand and cunning or crafty on the other. *Webster's New World Dictionary* defines the word "prudent" as "capable of exercising sound judgment in practical matters, especially as concerns one's own interests." Not being able to discern the difference between good and evil, Adam and Eve would not have contemplated any of the creatures under their authority as being evil-minded toward them. Therefore they would have innocently, and perhaps naively, viewed the serpent as one who is prudent. The question as to whether the serpent was providing sound judgment or deceitful advice would never have entered their minds. Who better to inform them about the ability to discern between good and evil than the one creature under their dominion they knew to be renown for its ability to exercise sound judgment in practical matters?

Nor would Adam or Eve think it strange or in any way unusual for a serpent, or any creature, to talk to them. They had no reason to be suspicious about the identity of the speaker or his intentions (Genesis 3:1-6). Either both were quite familiar with this form of communication with the creatures over which they exercised dominion or they were acquainted with the practice of angels speaking to them through these subordinate creatures. The former is the more likely scenario because deception is involved. Satan could have approached them directly and attempted to convince them to disobey God, much like what he did with Jesus in the wilderness. It was unsuccessful with Jesus and probably would have been unsuccessful with Adam and Eve. This is primarily because Adam and Eve were not given authority and dominion over the angels. Without this authority, they may have questioned the veracity of the statements of Satan if spoken to them directly.

In addition, the order of God's creation was perfect and good (Genesis 1:31). Before mankind's fall, there very well may have been this form of communication between Adam and Eve and the creatures of the earth. In Genesis 1:24, all animal life on earth is referred to as *nepesh chayah* ("living creatures"), which is the same Hebrew phrase used for man in Genesis 2:7. The main distinction between the two is that the animals were each made after its own kind, whereas man was made in the image and after the likeness of God.

There is nothing in the Holy Scriptures to indicate that all living creatures under Adam and Eve's dominion could not communicate with them. There is a scriptural reference to an occasion in which a living creature spoke to a person. It is located in Numbers 22:1-35. The colloquy between Balaam and his donkey was made possible because God "opened the mouth of the ass." It is important to note that these verses indicate that the donkey was a female (Numbers 22:28, 33) who spoke to Balaam from a first-person perspective (Numbers 22:28-30). No spiritual being possessed the donkey and spoke through it because, as previously noted, the angels are always referred to in the masculine sense. Not only was the animal able to hold its own conversation with Balaam, it could see the angel without having to have its eyes opened (Numbers 22:27, 33).

Balaam, however, had to have his eyes opened in order for him to see the angel (Numbers 22:31). This implies that Adam and Eve were initially able to see spiritual angels but had their spiritual eyes closed, apparently upon their fall from grace. If this were true, Adam and Eve would have been able to see God and the hosts of heaven, including Satan, before their fall. The only way for Satan to conceal his presence was to possess the serpent. It also implies that the mouths of all animals were initially open to commune with mankind, but were closed at some point in time; again, most likely upon the fall of man. Adam and Eve's sin caused all of the physical realm to lose some measure of its perfection, and caused them to lose all of their spiritual abilities, which included their ability to see God and to directly communicate with the creatures over which they exercised dominion.

Nothing can be opened unless it was first closed. Nothing can be closed unless it was first open. If animals were indeed able to speak to us, they would be able to express their own thoughts, opinions, and feelings just as the donkey did to Balaam. Nothing in these passages suggests that Balaam was the least bit surprised upon hearing his donkey speak. He immediately answered it and held a brief conversation with it. If all living creatures on the earth were initially capable of communicating with each other, this would more than explain why Adam and Eve did not find it peculiar that a serpent was conversing with them.

When faced with the apparent contradiction between God's word and the word of the serpent, Adam and Eve chose the later. They did not recognize the fact that one of their subservient creatures was possessed by Satan, one of the greatest angels created by God, who purposed tremendous ill will toward them. Adam and Eve, in their innocence, could not contemplate a creature under their dominion disrespecting their authority by lying to them.

Adam and Eve had every reason to believe the serpent because, without Satan's instigation, the serpent would never have sought to deceive them into disobeying God.

Upon hearing Satan's deceiving words through the serpent, Eve focused on the Tree of the Knowledge of Good and Evil. She saw that the tree was good for food; pleasant to the eyes, and to be desired to make one wise (Genesis 3:6). The Holy Spirit's description of Eve's perception of this tree gives us insight into what led to her and Adam's sin and, ultimately, the sins of all mankind.

All temptation can be categorized into three general but fundamental areas of life: (1) the lust of the flesh; (2) the lust of the eyes; and (3) the pride of life (1 John 2:16). The lust of the flesh includes all physical desires. The lust of the eyes relates to all personal desires. The pride of life concerns all manner of self-interests. When we give in to any of these three forms of temptation, whether overtly or subvertly in our hearts, our actions or thoughts give birth to sin; and when sin is full-grown, it gives birth to death (James 1:14-15).

Interestingly, when God created the Garden of Eden on earth, He made every tree in the Garden to be good for food and pleasant to the sight (Genesis 2:9). This included the Tree of Life and the Tree of the Knowledge of Good and Evil. As Adam and Eve were allowed to eat from every tree in the Garden, except the Tree of the Knowledge of Good and Evil (Genesis 2:16-17, 3:2-3), it was not sin for them to fulfill their physical and personal desires in this manner. Indeed, it is reasonable to conclude that Adam and Eve ate from various trees in the Garden except these two trees, constantly yielding to the lusts of their flesh and eyes on numerous occasions prior to Satan's deception.

Since God allowed them to indulge these two lusts, to fill their stomachs and please their eyes, Adam and Eve may not have considered it deserving of death to satisfy these lusts by eating from the Tree of the Knowledge of Good and Evil, despite God's warning to the contrary. They were obviously mistaken because the test was for them to demonstrate their uncompromising love for God. This kind of love does not need to be justified or earned. It is the same kind of love that Jesus obediently demonstrated to His Father and to every one of us by giving up His life so that we may be saved.

Any attempt by Adam and Eve to justify their actions would indicate that they missed the point of God's commandment not to eat from the forbidden tree. In any event, they couldn't blame their actions on ignorance because they gave in to the forbidden third form of lust; namely, the pride of life. Up to this point in their earthly existence, Adam and Eve had never attempted to satisfy their pride of life. If there was any credence to the argument that their eating the fruit of the Tree of the Knowledge of Good and Evil to fill their stomachs and to please their eyes, though forbidden, should not be deserving of death because they did not fully comprehend the reason for the prohibition and because they had been satisfying these lusts all along, that argument becomes moot when they ate from this forbidden tree to satisfy their pride of life. Adam and Eve were never permitted by God to satisfy this form of lust. In order for them to satisfy this third form of lust, Adam and Eve had to knowingly and intentionally place their love of self over their love of God. Their pride in who they were and what they could become through disobedience overwhelmed any love they had for the God Who created them. According to Proverbs 16:18, pride goes before destruction and a haughty spirit before a fall. Satan's sin of pride is an excellent illustration of this adage (Isaiah 14:12-13). The same fate befell Adam and Eve.

Satan, through the serpent, tempted Adam and Eve in all three of these ways. They did not have to disobey God and eat from the Tree of the Knowledge of Good and Evil to satisfy the first two types of lustful desires because they could have done so by eating from any of the other trees in the Garden. Doing so, knowing that it was against the commandment of God, was a clear statement of their willingness to defy God; and that statement served to be their death knell. Adam and Eve in essence made a choice between life and death: life through obedience or death through disobedience. In the end, every human being will have to choose between life (in and through God, through unconditional and uncompromising obedient love) or death (separate and apart from God, through selfish disobedience). There is no better illustration of this than the story of Lot's wife, who suffered a horrible death because she missed her worldly life so much that, in direct disobedience of God, she looked back upon the destruction of Sodom and Gomorrah.

When Eve saw that the fruit of the Tree of the Knowledge of Good and Evil was to be desired to make one wise, she was overcome by her desire to have that Godly attribute she believed would make her like God, even though God forbade her from eating of the fruit of this tree. Eve's covetousness caused her to give in to her desire to satisfy her self-interests, and she ate of the forbidden fruit not so much to feed herself or to satisfy the lust of her eyes, but to have what she knew she couldn't have—to satisfy her pride of life. It appears, from a literal reading of Genesis 3:6, that Adam was nearby at the time of Satan's deception of Eve because the verse says "she took of the fruit thereof, and did eat, and gave also unto her husband with her; and he did eat." This verse implies that, while Eve was the only one of the two actually deceived by Satan (Genesis 3:13; 1 Timothy 2:14), Adam, through Eve, was also the indirect recipient of all three temptations and ate for the same reasons that Eve ate of the fruit of the forbidden tree (Genesis 3:17). Adam also must have seen that the Tree of the Knowledge of Good and Evil was good for food, pleasing to the eyes and to be desired to make one wise. Like Eve, Adam also must have knowingly decided to choose life without God instead of life in and through God.

Upon observing Eve's sin of disobedience, Adam was faced with three courses of action. First, he could have prevented Eve from eating of the tree. He could have been adamant about it, leaving her no other option but to disobey her husband as well as God if she wanted to eat from the tree. Eve, being created from the rib of Adam (Genesis 2:21-22), was extremely devoted to her husband, perhaps more so than to God. It is doubtful that she would have rebelled against her husband to satisfy her lusts.

Second, Adam could have refused to give in to the temptations despite Eve's sinful actions, much like what Jesus did when He was similarly tempted by Satan in the wilderness (Luke 4:1-12) despite our sins against God. Had Adam withstood these temptations, he could have interceded on Eve's behalf before God and, if necessary, died in her stead. His sinless death would have been an atonement for her sins, restoring her to her original estate with God. God would have surely resurrected Adam just like He resurrected Jesus, who was later required to offer His divine sinless life for the sins of not only Adam and Eve but all mankind. Finally, Adam could have chosen to join Eve in the satiation of their lusts. Unfortunately for all of us, he chose the latter of the three options before him.

Adam and Eve had to know of the existence of the Tree of Life in the Garden. They had to fully understand the peculiar natures of both the Tree of Life and the Tree of the Knowledge of Good and Evil. They had to know that eating from the Tree of Life would cause the partaker thereof to live forever (Genesis 3:22). The Scriptures suggest that the fruit of the Tree of Life gave the partaker thereof wisdom and discretion (Proverbs 3:13-26). They had to know that eating from the Tree of the Knowledge of Good and Evil would cause the partaker thereof to be able to know the difference between good and evil (Genesis 3:6;22). They had to fully appreciate everything relating to the power of these two trees because the Garden of Eden was located on the earth and thus came under their authority and dominion.

They could have chosen the Tree of Life and received eternal life (Genesis 3:22), but they reasoned that eternal life without this missing Godly attribute would leave them eternally that much less than their Creator. By choosing to disobey God, Adam and Eve intentionally chose their own way to be like God over God's way. They sought to unilaterally improve their position in God's order of things by eating of the forbidden fruit and then securing forever their newly obtained forbidden attribute by eating of the fruit from the Tree of Life. God protected Adam and Eve from themselves. God kept them from eating from the Tree of Life, which would have allowed them to live forever in their sinful state. God therefore drove them out of paradise and placed angelic guards at the East gate of the Garden of Eden, and a flaming sword to deny them access to the Tree of Life (Genesis 3:22-24).

Upon their fall through their sin of disobedience, Adam and Eve were denied the perfection of their ill-gotten evil ways. Their God-given power and authority left them upon their separation from Him through sin. When this occurred, they realized that they could never truly wield any power and authority independent of God. This same power and authority was later given to Jesus upon His sacrificial death and resurrection (Matthew 28:18). As a result, all who accept, in faith, the death and resurrection of Jesus Christ for the forgiveness of their sins will have this power and authority not only restored unto them but also perfected.

Satan deceived Adam and Eve into believing that if they disobeyed God and ate of the Tree of the Knowledge of Good and Evil, they would be like God. Little did Adam and Eve know that they were created not just to be like God but to become one with God. They were made in God's image and after His likeness so that God could abide in them and they in God. Had they eaten of the Tree of Life prior to this deception and their sin, they would have become so much more than like God. They would have become one with God, to the same extent that Jesus is one with His Father. They would have received wisdom and discretion, the very Godly attributes they were theretofore missing.

What greater deception could Satan have used but to convince Adam and Eve into obtaining, through disobedience, what they were already freely offered through obedience? They did not know that what they sought to become on their own against God's will was what God had intended them to actually be in His will. Adam and Eve sought to be separate but equal to God. God wanted them to be one with Him. They wanted to be like God. God wanted to abide in and through them and for them to abide in and through Him; a condition so much better than being like God. Adam and Eve treasured love of self. God wanted them to treasure love of their Creator. They did not know that they were destined to receive the power, glory and wisdom of God, which is now available to all of us who are called by God (1 Corinthians 1:24).

The Consequences of the Sin of Adam and Eve

Adam and Eve willingly sinned in every way a person can sin. They gave in to all of the three basic forms of human temptations. The extent of their sin has set the standard for the sins of all their descendants throughout time. The sin nature of all mankind, which is not of God and permeates the world, causes all of us to consistently give in to these three types of temptations (1 John 2:16). We cannot resist our sin nature (Romans 7:15-23).

Adam and Eve's choice was between life in and through God, and knowledge of good and evil through an existence separate and apart from God. Had they chosen the former, they would have lived as temples of their Holy God whose life would have become their life. No one can have life independent of God's life. If they had eaten from the Tree of Life before sinning, their sinless nature would have been perfected and they would never have known sin, just as Jesus never knew sin (2 Corinthians 5:21). A person cannot be one with God and know sin. To commit sin requires the absence of love. By choosing to eat from the Tree of the Knowledge of Good and Evil, Adam and Eve demonstrated that they lacked the kind of love that is of God. Instead, they cold-heartedly chose an existence apart from God wherein they could choose to do good or evil as the lusts of their hearts so determined. They would experience both good and evil and, hence, know them. The ramifications of their sin of disobedience meant that they would have no life at all.

Satan succeeded in persuading Adam and Eve to yield to their lusts and eat of the fruit from the forbidden tree first. His participation in God's obedience test of Adam and Eve was allowed by God to determine if they would overcome temptation with obedient love. This test unfortunately evidenced the fact that every one of us, if given the choice in an innocent state, would succumb to our own lusts instead of obeying God.

Before their fall, there was no sin in Adam and Eve; thus they could not die. They were told that disobedience to God is the only way they could suffer death (Genesis 2:16-17). By rejecting God, Adam and Eve were deserving of death, for God said: "For in the day that thou eatest thereof thou shalt surely die" (Genesis 2:17). We know that death can be both physical and spiritual. Physical death is the separation of the spirit from the body (James 2:26). Spiritual death is the eternal separation of the individual spirit from God, resulting in eternal damnation in the lake of fire (Revelation 20:14; 21:8).

Chapter 3 of the book of Genesis, on its face, indicates that Adam and Eve did not immediately suffer either of these two forms of death as a result of their sin. God does not lie, and He didn't lie here. God's choice of words in this warning is telling. He said "in the day," not "on the day." The use of the preposition "in" here denotes "at some point during a period of time." As we discussed earlier, from God's perspective, a day is as a thousand years, and a thousand years is as one day (2 Peter 3:8). No man has ever lived for more than 999 years. The oldest person identified in the Bible is Methuselah, who lived 969 years (Genesis 5:27).

Genesis 5:5 tells us that Adam lived 930 years. According to God's time, Adam did not live for more than one day and did indeed die "at some point during the day" that he ate of the forbidden fruit. God's word was true. The Bible is silent as to when Eve died, and so there is every reason to believe that she also did not live for more than one day (according to God's perspective of time) and died "in the day" that she ate of the forbidden fruit. Thus, both Adam and Eve suffered both physical and spiritual death because their spirits, once separated from their bodies as a result of physical death, were not allowed to be with God. They were kept in Abraham's bosom (Luke 16:22) until Jesus' ascension, when He led captivity captive (Ephesians 4:8-10). The death sentence promised by God not only applied to Adam and Eve but also to their descendants.

God's Covenant with Adam and Eve

There is an inseparable connection between mankind and all temporal creation. This can be gleaned from the Word of God because the universe and everything in it lost its perfection with the fall of Adam and Eve (Genesis 3:17-18; Romans 8:19, 22). Before mankind's fall, all creatures lived in harmony feeding on the land instead of each other. After the millennial reign of Christ, all creatures shall once again return to this state of perfect harmony (Isaiah 65:17-25). It is interesting to note that Satan's sin, and the sins of the fallen angels, did not adversely affect the universe. Only the fall of man directly affected the entire universe. Our redemption is critical to the restoration of the universe to its original state of perfection. As we go, so goes the universe.

God, who is Spirit, intended that He would live in and through us, a feat which could not be accomplished through spiritual angels, who cannot have a material, temporal existence and are created to be ministering spirits (Hebrews 1:14). In order for God to achieve His intended purpose for us and all of creation, we had to be redeemed.

Jesus' death and resurrection has permanently resolved all the consequences of our sins and has enabled us to be restored to our original state of perfection. Once this restoration is complete, the universe will also return to its original, perfect state (2 Peter 3:7, 10-13; Revelation 21:1-6). Jesus, who is God in man and man in God, sustains the universe (Colossians 1:17). We, who will become one with Jesus, will also have God in us, and we will be in God because our living triune Godhead will indwell us and we will indwell Them. We will be mirror images of Them. Being one with our triune Godhead, we will share in the responsibility of sustaining the universe as we were originally intended to do. Until we are resurrected in glory, we may never fully understand the interdependent relationship we share with all of God's creation.

God, in His infinite mercy, offered Adam and Eve a promise of complete atonement for their sin in the first messianic prophecy of the Bible, which is contained in Genesis 3:15. God promised that they would be physically and spiritually restored to their original estate. In verse 20 of that same chapter, Adam takes his first act of faith in furtherance of God's promise of salvation unto eternal life by naming his wife "Eve," which comes from the verb "to live." God acknowledged Adam's act of faith by covering their sin symbolically through the shedding of blood and physically covering their nakedness with coats of skin or tunics (Genesis 3:21).

God had to shed the innocent blood of one of His creatures to temporarily physically and spiritually cover Adam and Eve. The Word of God doesn't indicate what kind of animal lost its life, but the innocent animal certainly did not deserve death as a result of the commission of Adam and Eve's sin. This is the first recorded death in the Holy Scriptures and it was at the hands of God. We do not know if Adam and Eve fully understood the prophetic significance of this symbolic covering by the shedding of innocent and unblemished blood. God would continue to require the periodic shedding of innocent, unblemished animal blood for the temporary atonement of man's sins until God shed His own innocent blood through His sinless and unblemished Son, Jesus Christ, so that all the sins of the world may be forever forgiven.

Every descendant of Adam and Eve who believes that God allowed part of Himself, His Living Word, to become flesh and to be sacrificed on the cross for the forgiveness of all of our sins, redeeming us to be finally glorified in His image and after His likeness, will be saved (1 John 5:4-5; Romans 8:29-30). The same is true for all those who never heard the gospel of salvation through Jesus Christ because their salvation is secured by their belief in God based upon their observance of all of creation that surrounds them (Romans 1:20). First John 3:2 tells us that when Jesus reappears, every saved person shall be like Him, for we shall be transformed into His image.

Though husband and wife in Eden, Adam and Eve were not allowed to conceive before the completion of their test. God knew that they would fail the test and would have to be put out of the Garden of Eden and conceive in pain. As a result, when mankind began to multiply on the earth, they were begotten in the image of man, after his own kind and not after God, much like all of God's other earthly creations (Genesis 1:21, 24-25; 5:1-3). Specifically, in Genesis 5:3 we are told that Adam "begat a son in his own likeness, after his image; and called his name Seth."

First Corinthians 15:45-49 tell us that just as we have borne the image of man, we shall also bear the image of the heavenly. In other words, we were born in Adam's fallen image, but God's promise to us is that we shall once again bear God's image and be in a position to fulfill our original creative purpose above all creation.

Despite Satan's initial successes in the enlistment of

mankind in his rebellion against God, we can collect on the redemptive promises of God by individually passing the eternal test of obedience through faith. Are you willing to dedicate the rest of your earthly life to a loving obedience to God in return for an eternity of oneness with Him? Our lives are but whispers in the wind, briefly heard and then remembered at best. The question each of us must now answer is whether, armed with the knowledge of our true creative purpose, we will choose to demonstrate our unconditional and uncompromising love for God or whether we will choose to demonstrate our hatred of Him by blatantly disobeying Him.

CHAPTER FOUR

THE REDEMPTION OF MAN

In the previous chapters, we have looked at the creative process, generally, and as it applies to us. We have also looked at the reason for Satan's rebellion against God, and Satan's deception of Adam and Eve. We have considered the consequences of Adam and Eve's disobedience to God, and God's promise of salvation for everyone who would accept it.

We shall now examine God's redemption of His highest creation and why God chose not to redeem the fallen angels. We shall see how God induced Satan, the father of deception, into deceiving himself into believing that he could destroy God's redemptive plan for us by persuading Jesus to become one with him through sin. His efforts to do so resulted in him performing the very acts that provided for our redemption.

God's Redemptive Plan for Mankind

We were created in the image and after the likeness of God and thereby given the Godly attributes necessary for us to become the children of God. Upon our glorification, as the redeemed sons and daughters of God who are one with their Father, we become the fourth personage of God. There will then be God the Father, God the Son, God the Holy Ghost, and God the Children as brethren of Christ. It is our creative purpose to become one with God to this unimaginable extent.

The Garden of Eden experience provided an opportunity for us to perfect our predestined position in God's ordered creation. Had Adam and Eve eaten from the Tree of Life instead of the Tree of the Knowledge of Good and Evil, they and their progeny would have perfected, through their demonstration of unconditional, uncompromising and loving obedience, this oneness with God forever. I will use these descriptive words often to present the kind of love which God is and which we must become before we can be one with Him. It was the kind of love God was seeking from Adam and Eve in the Garden of Eden. This type of loving obedience required them to be content to glorify God by being that which they were created to be, even if they didn't completely understand the full extent of their creative purpose. It required them to give up all self-interests and desires to the extent that they contradicted God's will. Adam and Eve had to trust that whatever God had in store for them, it would allow them to function at their maximum creative potential. It is only when we place obedience to God above our personal interests and desires that God's interests and desires can co-exist with us. In essence, we have to give up any desire to have a life independent from God in order for us to gain eternal life in and through God.

Unfortunately, when given the choice between (1)

giving up self-identity and allowing God to live in and through them and (2) existing separate from God but constantly seeking to be like God, Adam and Eve chose the latter. As a result, this desire to be like, but separate from, God has been ingrained in our nature since their fall from grace.

Having succumbed to Satan's temptation to disobey God's command not to eat from the Tree of the Knowledge of Good and Evil, they deserved and were destined for death via separation from God. This death would not only be a physical separation, it would also be a spiritual one; and both would be eternal in duration. If this were to happen, God would have to abandon His plan of becoming one with and physically manifesting Himself through his greatest creation. Satan's deception therefore would have resulted in every human being becoming eternally one with him instead of with God, and therefore doomed to share in his eternal damnation and separation from God. Satan had every reason to assume that we would be forever removed from our first estate just like he was.

However, God would not allow Satan to profit from his rebellious pride. But if we were not to die for our sins, someone would have to die in our place. Our creation was the climatic event of creation week. No other creature held an estate equal to or higher than us, much to the consternation of Satan. If we were to be pardoned from our death sentences, there was but one entity who could die in our place and that was God Himself. So God purposed to have His Living Word, the second personage of our triune Godhead through Whom He spoke into existence the universe (Hebrews 1:2) and through Whom all creation consists (Colossians 1:16-

17), to become flesh (John 1:14) and die in our place. Because of our sins we are deserving of death. Through the death of Jesus Christ, Who knew no sin and Who was undeserving of death, we are relieved of our death penalties.

In 1 John 2:12, it is written:

> I write unto you, little children, because your sins are forgiven *you* for his name's sake. (Emphasis added)

The apostle John implies in this passage that, although the world has been forgiven for their sins to the glorification of God's name, there is still a requirement of death for the commission of those sins. That is why it says "your sins are forgiven you" instead of "your sins are forgiven." The addition of the word "you" in this verse signifies that some blameless person will be held accountable for the sins of the world in our place. We are forgiven of our sins and thereby released from our death penalties because Jesus was that blameless person Who satisfied God's requirement that the consequences of our sins be fulfilled.

Since the life of the flesh is in the blood, and the wages of sin is death, our redemption and restoration could only be achieved if there was a shedding of blood unto physical and spiritual death. For it is written:

> And almost all things are by the law purged with blood; and without shedding of blood is no remission. (Hebrews 9:22)

It had to be the shedding unto death of blood from a sinless person because the death of a sinful person cannot pay for the sins of others, since his death would be the consequence of his own sins. More importantly, it also had to be the shedding unto death of blood that contained eternal life, so that the sins of the world could be forgiven. Only God's eternal life-giving blood was available to pay the death penalties for all the sins of mankind. Jesus' sacrificial, sinless death was endured not only for God's elect, but also for the sins of the whole world (Luke 2:32; John 1:29). In 1 John 2:2, it is written:

> And he is the propitiation for our sins: and not for ours only, but also for the sins of the whole world.

This means that every human being ever to be born of Adam and Eve had his or her death penalty paid by the death and resurrection of Jesus the Christ. The shedding of Jesus' eternal, life-giving blood unto death and His ensuing three-day physical and spiritual separation from God was sufficient for the propitiation of the sins of any person who accepts this sacrifice, in faith, being reconciled unto God. (2 Corinthians 5:19).

In order for God's blood to be shed for the sins of mankind, He had to have a human body. This was accomplished by the Holy Spirit impregnating Mary, whose sinful flesh gave birth to Jesus. Jesus is the only person who was capable of redeeming mankind because, though He was born with the sinful nature of Adam and Eve through His mother, Mary, He is also God and therefore born with a sinless nature. He is human and yet impeccable.

Just as God permitted Satan to tempt Adam and Eve in the Garden of Eden, He also permitted Jesus to be

similarly tempted by Satan in the wilderness where
Jesus fasted for forty days (Luke 4:2). Anyone who has
ever fasted from food knows that during the fast you are
continually tempted to give in to one or more of the
three fundamental areas of lusts. You will be tempted to
break your fast by satisfying (1) your lust of the flesh
(i.e., hunger); (2) your lust of your eyes (i.e., delectable
food); or (3) your pride of life (i.e., putting your self-
interests before the fast). Anyone who has fasted also
knows that forty days of eating nothing will test one's
resolve against these lusts to the absolute maximum.
The Holy Scriptures contain two other references where
individuals fasted for forty days and forty nights. Moses
did so on Mount Sinai (Exodus 24:18; 34:28;
Deuteronomy 9:9-25), and Elijah did so on Mount
Horeb (1 Kings 19:8).

Luke 4:1-2 tell us that Jesus, being full of the Holy
Spirit, was led by the Spirit into the wilderness where
He fasted forty days. The Holy Spirit isolated Jesus so
that He could focus on the supreme test of loving
obedience to God, just as Adam and Eve were isolated
in the Garden of Eden when they were similarly tested.
These verses state that throughout the entire forty-day
fast Jesus was so tested by the devil.

These tests involved each of the three areas of
temptation in which Adam and Eve were tested and the
intensities of these tests no doubt increased as the fast
progressed. After the forty-day fast had ended, but
before Jesus had an opportunity to replenish Himself,
Satan tempted Jesus one last time in each of the three
aforementioned areas of temptation. Satan specifically
tested Jesus' hunger; visions of worldly power and
glory; and sense of self-pride. Jesus' successful

resistance of these three fundamental forms of temptation throughout His earthly life and sacrificial death and resurrection has placed Him in a position to aid all who are similarly tempted (Hebrews 2:18).

Satan knew that Jesus was another form of Adam, a progenitor of the spiritually reborn children of God much like Adam was the forefather of mankind. Through the wilderness temptations, Satan sought to entice Jesus into sinning against God, thereby removing any apparent hope of our spiritual rebirths. Despite Satan's best efforts Jesus never sinned.

By lovingly choosing God's interests and desires over His own, Jesus was given eternal life not just for Himself but for all of mankind who would choose to do the same thing on the faith of Jesus' promises. Had Jesus given in to any of these three forms of temptation, He would have placed Himself above the will of God and would have shown that His love of God was conditional and secondary to His love of self. He would have therefore sinned against God. But praise be to God, unlike Adam and Eve, Jesus passed all three tests (Luke 4:1-13).

To have undergone forty days of this type of intense temptation while depriving the body of all of its essential needs, and yet never sinning, is a testament to the limitless faith of God and the complete and total freedom from sin that we can enjoy if we allow God to abide in us to the extent God abides in Jesus.

The death of Jesus, the Word of God Who became the sinless Son of God and Whose blood contained eternal life, brought about the redemption of all sinful flesh who are spiritually reborn into this sinless state. There are three Greek words used in the New Testament to describe the redemption of the children of God. One such word is *agorazo*, which means "to purchase in the market" (Revelation 5:9; 14:3-4). Another is *exagorazo*, which means "to purchase and take home" (Galatians 3:13). The last word is *lutroo,* which means "to purchase and give freedom" (Luke 24:21; 1 Peter 1:18). Through the blood of Jesus Christ, all of mankind were purchased, brought home and set free from their captivity to sin and its accompanying death sentence.

However, our redemption would not be imposed on us, just as the eternal union with God in Eden was never imposed on Adam and Eve. When they elected to become like God through disobedience, they in essence chose not to accept that initial free gift. Now that same gift is, again, freely available to every person who will accept it. Unlike Adam and Eve, we have an informed choice.

We are all familiar with the story of the prodigal son as set forth in Luke 15:11-32. I once heard a radio message, given by a preacher whose name I cannot now recall, that enlightened my understanding of this parable. Apparently, it was the custom of those times that the father would seriously rebuke any child who prematurely sought his inheritance in this fashion because it would be interpreted to be a statement that the child could not wait for his father to die to get what would then be his rightful inheritance. If the father neglected to rebuke the son, the eldest son would have surely stepped in to do what the father failed to do.

However, in this story, the father divided up the inheritance and gave it to both sons. The father exhibited a tremendous degree of unconditional and uncompromising love to both sons. He allowed his youngest son to disrespect him and leave his presence with his portion of the inheritance, and his oldest son to quietly take his portion of the inheritance though the father had not yet died. By their actions, both sons demonstrated that they were lost because they placed their own self-interests above the interests of their father.

When the youngest son repented and made his way back home, he had to know that the custom of the times also required him to be stoned to death for his disrespectful actions upon his return. He had every reason to believe that he was coming home to a death sentence. Thus, he was willing to give up any claims to heirship and live as a servant with no rights or privileges.

However, his father, even though his son was a great way off, ran to him and welcomed him back into his arms before his son could utter a request for forgiveness. In fact, the father does not respond to his son's confession of sin. Instead, he commands that his son be restored to his former position, with all of the rights and benefits of an heir, and that a feast be prepared. The oldest son appears to have been similarly forgiven. The father's unconditional and uncompromising love for both sons is an excellent example of the degree of love God has for each one of us despite our continuing disrespect for Him through our commission of sin. God welcomes back all who are repentant; God forgives them and completely restores them. Our restoration, however, came at a price. God had to take His love for us to a level higher than that of the father of the prodigal sons. He had to become man and pay our death penalties reserved for us because of our sins.

The oneness with God that Adam and Eve enjoyed before their fall was but a precursor to the indivisibility we shall experience when we become one with Him in glory (Philippians 3:21; Colossians 3:4). Jesus is the personification of man being one with God in glory. All of the children of God will be conformed into the glorious image of Jesus Christ (Romans 8:29-30; 2 Corinthians 3:18), who is the express image of the heavenly God (Hebrews 1:3). God's ultimate plan to become forever one in glory with His highest creation could never be permanently thwarted by Satan.

If we will accept, in faith, God's death on our behalf for the propitiation of our sins, we will be spiritually reborn and physically resurrected unto eternal life just as God resurrected Himself, in the person of Jesus Christ, from death. In John 1:12 it is written:

> But as many as received him, to them gave he power to become the sons of God, even to them that believe on his name.

When Jesus returns, we will be given incorruptible bodies. When this happens, our oneness with God will be perfected, in answer to Jesus' prayer, and God's chosen of mankind will abide in Him and He in them. It is impossible for us to fully envision just what it will be like to be one with God; yet this is exactly what the Word of God tells us we will become if we are the children of God.

God's Eternal Perspective of Man's Redemption

From God's perspective, everything happens at once. God is not restricted by any temporal limitations.

He is the beginning and the end; both at the same time (Psalm 90:2; Revelation 1:8, 11; 21:6; 22:13). All eternity occurs simultaneously from God's perspective. This would explain how Jesus, Who is God and Who is the same and will remain the same forever (Hebrews 13:8), could be slain from the foundation of the world (Revelation 13:8) from an eternal perspective, and yet, from our temporal perspective, undergo that fate 2,000 years ago.

Knowing the hearts of men, God looked out over time and identified all of mankind who would be receptive to His free offer of salvation and wrote their names in the Book of Life from the foundation of the world (Revelation 17:8).

From God's perspective, He continues to experience an eternity of complete and total oneness with every one of His children who were spared from the wages of their sins by the death and resurrection of Jesus Christ even though that reality has yet to be experienced by us. We shall one day be able to experience the simultaneity of God. In that state of co-existence with God, all that will happen from the beginning to the end of all things will be simultaneously experienced by God and us. From that point on, nothing will be new to us.

For it is written in Ecclesiastes 1:9:

> The thing that hath been, it is that which shall be;
> and that which is done is that which shall be done:
> and there is no new thing under the sun.

From our current standpoint, the names of the saved are written in the Book of Life at the very moment of their salvation and spiritual rebirths through acceptance of our Lord Jesus as their Savior. Our temporal existence will not allow for us to experience the past or the future at the same time that we experience the present. We live in the faith and the hope that God's perspective will become our perspective. We should have unwavering faith in what the future will hold for us because, from God's eternal perspective, it has already occurred.

God's master plan to redeem us, through the sacrificial blood of Jesus Christ, Who came to seek and to save that which was lost (Luke 19:10), was therefore completed by God from the foundation of the world (Hebrews 4:3). However, to us, it is being carried out over the span of millennia.

This interrelationship between the eternal and the temporal is demonstrated when our prayers are answered. Our prayers, which are made over time, are heard and answered from God's eternal perspective. From His perspective, a name can be written in the Book of Life before the foundation of the world as a direct result of the fervent prayer of a child of God today or at any time since the foundation of the world because it all happens at once.

One of the first multimillion-dollar verdicts I was involved with occurred relatively early in my legal career. I was one of three attorneys from our firm who were assigned a group of three plaintiffs, each allegedly suffering from an asbestos-related cancer; two lung and one laryngeal. Their cases were to be tried in Washington, D.C. and so we secured living arrangements there. As God would have it, I was assigned the laryngeal case, which was the most difficult to prove.

The defendants in my case filed a motion to have my

client's case dismissed pursuant to a D.C. statute which they argued required dismissal of a products liability action where the plaintiff waits more than one year from the date he first misses work due to a work-related injury to sue an entity whose negligence was alleged to have caused the injury. My client's case was filed more than one year after he first missed work due to the development of laryngeal cancer allegedly caused by his occupational exposure to asbestos. He had missed six months from work due to his cancer. The court set a deadline for me to establish why my client's case should not be dismissed. We had every reason to believe that the statute was applicable.

The D.C. statute was derived from a California statute. I attended law school in Los Angeles, and still maintained contact with some of my law school colleagues. I contacted one of them and requested an annotated version of the applicable California statute. I did not hear back from him and the day of the deadline arrived without any meaningful research results.

The morning of the court hearing, I arose from bed, got on my knees, and asked God, Who knew the hearts of everyone involved, to take this matter from me and let His will be done. Almost immediately I was overcome with a sense of joy and relief. There was no stress. It was no longer my concern. It was His to do with as he pleased. Keep in mind that I was but a few hours away from having my client's case dismissed, and I knew of no legal reason why that should not be my client's fate. Yet I had this indescribable inner peace.

About an hour later I was moved to call the home office. Upon doing so, I was informed that I had received a fax. I had it forwarded to the copy center across the street and walked there to pick it up. It was a copy of the annotated code of the California statute which established that the one-year statute of limitations did not begin to run unless or until the worker was unable to return to work. As my client returned to work after a six-month recovery period, his case could not be dismissed. I could hardly contain my excitement. Upon receipt of this research, the court denied the motion and my client went on to win a $9 million verdict, millions more than the other two plaintiffs who received verdicts of 4 and 2.5 million, respectively.

What took days to unfold from my perspective occurred simultaneously from God's eternal perspective. The Holy Spirit, Who dwells in me, allowed me to experience the joy of victory before it actually occurred from my perspective because it had already happened from His perspective.

Once we obtain eternal life with and in God through Christ Jesus, God's timeless existence will be our timeless existence. Thousands of years will be as days to us, and days like thousands of years. Through and in our Father, we shall be both the beginning and the end, the Alpha and the Omega.

No Salvation for the Fallen Angels

Hebrews 2:16 tells us that Jesus Christ took not the nature of angels, but the seed of Abraham. From this verse, it must be concluded that, for reasons unknown to us, God chose to redeem Adam and Eve and those of their descendants who are called by God to Himself, but not the fallen angels (2 Peter 2:4). Why were the angels not offered the gift of eternal salvation? Perhaps it was because Adam and Eve sinned before they fully understood and appreciated all of the benefits and responsibilities associated with their first estate; whereas the fallen angels fully understood all these things and yet sinned nonetheless.

Adam and Eve, in their innocent state, had yet to experience oneness with God in incorruptible bodies that could not sin, a position for which they were created. Unaware of this fact, they chose to attain this eternal God-like status through disobedience. They were never able to fully appreciate all that they were created to be because they sinned before they were glorified by becoming eternally one with God. Atonement can be had for sins done in ignorance (*bishgagah*) (Leviticus 4:2-35). In fact, Jesus said shortly before He died on the cross: "Father, forgive them; for they know not what they do" (Luke 23:34).

Satan and his angels were all they were going to be and sinned presumptuously because they wanted to be more. In Numbers 15:30, it is written:

> But the soul that doeth aught presumptuously, whether he be born in the land, or a stranger, the same reproacheth the LORD; and that soul shall be cut off from among his people.

The word "presumptuously" in this verse literally means "with a high hand." In other words, raising one's hands in defiance of and against God. If a person would not be forgiven should he defiantly blaspheme the Lord (Hebrews 10:26-28), surely an angel who takes up arms against the Holy Spirit would not be forgiven. Satan and his angels, being spiritual entities, engaged in a spiritual rebellion against the Spirit of God. God, in His mercy, will forgive a sin against Him but not a sin against His

Holy Spirit (Isaiah 63:10; Matthew 12:31-32; Mark 3:29; Luke 12:10; Acts 5:3-4, 9; 7:51; Hebrews 10:29).

It could also have been that Adam and Eve ate from the Tree of the Knowledge of Good and Evil, and thus they knew both good and evil. Should our evil nature be redeemed, we would know only good and have only a good nature. The fallen angels, however, never ate from this tree and therefore only knew evil because of their sin. Since they did not know good, there were no redeeming qualities in the fallen angels. Salvation was not an option.

Finally, God in His infinite mercy was willing to allow a part of Himself to become one of us by supernaturally causing His Holy Word to become flesh through Mary and, though sinless, take on the sins of the world and satisfy the death penalties associated with them. God was thereby able to separate Himself from His only begotten Son, for a time through physical and spiritual death, for the salvation of mankind because Jesus, as man, possessed His own body and soul that could be separated from God. The angels do not possess physical bodies. Thus, the salvation of the angels would have required the purely spiritual separation of God from Himself unto spiritual death. God cannot spiritually die by separating Himself from Himself. For it is written,

> Every kingdom divided against itself is brought to desolation; and every city or house divided against itself shall not stand: And if Satan cast out Satan, he is divided against himself; how shall then his kingdom stand? (Matthew 12:25-26)

These angels were doomed to suffer death, through

eternal separation from God, for their sins.

For whatever reasons, God decided not to redeem the fallen angels. Instead, these angels, with the exception of those angels who left their estate to sleep with the daughters of men (Genesis 6:1-4; Jude 6), are allowed by God to perform the ministerial function of determining who among us would either accept His free offer of eternal life or choose their own way unto death. These fallen angels serve a vital role in this selective process because they continually tempt us to be our own god instead of allowing God to exist in and through us. It could be argued that each of these fallen angels are cherubim because their ministerial service to God involves the judgment of man. Surviving the travails of these tests, through obedience, draws those called by God closer to Him. It is our demonstration of loving obedience to God during these tests which allows us to be separated as wheat from the chaff.

Satan's Self-Deception

As previously discussed, the only way for our sinless God to die in our place was for Him to become man. The Living Word of God was made flesh, and we beheld His glory (John 1:14). He is the every utterance of God, and He became God's only begotten Son (John 1:18; 1 John 4:9). Some manuscripts interpret the phrase "only begotten Son" as "only begotten God." In fact, in Isaiah 9:6, the prophet states that the child, who is given unto us, is called *El Gib-bohr* meaning "The Mighty God" or "God Hero." Jesus became both God and man from the moment of His conception. Thus He is the express image of God (2 Corinthians 4:4; Hebrews 1:2-3) because the Spirit of God abides in Him. Yet Jesus was susceptible to all of the sins of the flesh, of the eyes, and of pride of life because He was made in the likeness of man (Romans 8:3-4; Philippians 2:7). As God, He was nonetheless able to remain sinless throughout His entire life.

Lest anyone think that it was easy for Jesus to live a sinless life for thirty-three years in this sinful world, the author of Hebrews tells us that in every way, shape, or fashion, Jesus' temptations were the same as ours:

> For we have not a high priest which cannot be touched with the feeling of our infirmities; but was in all points tempted like as we are, yet without sin. (Hebrews 4:15)
> Who in the days of his flesh, when he had offered up prayers and supplications with strong crying and tears unto him that was able to save him from death, and was heard in that he feared; Though he were a Son, yet learned he obedience by the things which he suffered; And being made perfect, he became the author of eternal salvation unto all them that obey him. (Hebrews 5:7-9)

The fact that Jesus was able to live in the flesh for thirty-three years without sinning begs the question: Why would Satan, being an intelligent creature, cause Jesus to experience a sinless death knowing that, as a result thereof, souls would be saved and he would be condemned? Perhaps Satan reasoned that no man could endure the suffering Jesus went through without sinning by cursing God orally or in his heart. Any sin on Jesus' part would have rendered His death the wages of His own sin and thus could not serve as a propitiation for the sins of anyone else, let alone the whole world. Assuming that this was, in fact, Satan's reasoning, it was woefully inaccurate. However, there are scriptural references that suggest that Satan may have been induced into a form of self-deception.

The story of Job is illustrative. Job lived in the land of Uz (Job 1:1) hundreds, if not thousands, of years before the birth of Jesus. During his time, Job was the only man on earth who was blameless before God and who shunned evil (Job 1:8; 2:3). Despite his sin of pride, Satan had a ministerial service to perform and thus was permitted to accompany other angelic beings when they presented themselves before God during Job's time (Job 1:6; 2:1). On two of these occasions, God asked Satan from whence he came, and Satan responded that he came from going to and fro in the earth and walking up and down in it (Job 1:7; 2:2). The Scriptures are silent as to the nature of Satan's activities while traversing the globe, but the nature of the service he was performing for God up to this point suggests that he was busy tempting mankind with the permission of God. On each of these two occasions, God brought the subject of Job to Satan's attention. God, Who knows all things, knew that Satan, who does not, would rely on his experience with Job when Satan encountered a later blameless man before God who shunned evil, namely Jesus Christ.

During the first angelic presentation before God, Satan told God that Job was blameless before Him only because God protected him. Satan proposed that Job would curse God to His face if that protection was removed and he be allowed to fill Job's life with great tragedy. So Satan was given permission to destroy all that Job had, including his children, but he could not touch the person of Job (Job 1:12). The test was to see if

Job would sin by cursing God to His face. Job was a wealthy and well-respected man with a wife, seven sons, three daughters, and many possessions (Job 1:2-3). Satan took the lives of his ten children and all of his earthly possessions through human, natural, and supernatural means (Job 1:13-22). This was possible because Satan, through the sin of Adam and Eve, had become one with sinful man, had usurped man's dominion and authority over nature, and had continued access to heaven seeking the judgment of mankind.

Interestingly, Satan did not take the life of Job's wife. By leaving Job's wife alive, Satan had a living soul, who has sinned, available to tempt Job to sin just as Satan had Eve to tempt Adam to sin. Yet, despite this great string of tragedies in his life, Job never sinned (Job 1:20-22).

It is unclear whether Job's sinless death, at this time, would have paid the death penalty for the sins of others. Obviously, it was not God's intention for Job to sacrifice his life in this manner because God told Satan that he could not take Job's life (Job 2:6).

On the occasion of the second angelic presentation before God, Job was again brought to Satan's attention by God. Satan further proposed that Job would yet curse God to His face if God would remove His protection of Job and allow Satan to attack the body of Job. Therefore Satan was given permission to inflict great physical and emotional pain and suffering upon the person of Job. Again, the test was to see if this would cause Job to sin by cursing God to His face. Job's wife, being a witness to Job's supposed fall from grace, told Job to curse God and die (Job 2:9).

This statement by his wife is telling because it implies that she believed that, in order for Job to die, he had to first sin. In this case, cursing God would be the means of his sin. Job certainly considered cursing God in one's heart to be a sin because he offered burnt sacrifices daily for his ten children, before their untimely deaths, to sanctify them just in case they may have sinned by cursing God in their hearts (Job 1:5). If it was indeed commonly believed at that time that a person could not suffer illness, tragedy or death unless or until he had sinned, this would partially explain why Job's three friends considered his sufferings the result of previous sins.

Job refused his wife's suggestion that he curse God and die at least with his lips (Job 2:10). This scriptural limitation of the extent of Job's sinlessness to that of his lips infers that Job sinned in his heart while subjected to Satan's intense persecution. This is to be distinguished from when Satan took everything from Job but did not touch Job because, on that occasion, Job never sinned with his lips or otherwise. We know that Job obviously sinned at some point because he tells God that he despises himself and repents in dust and ashes (Job 42:6) and because Job ultimately died (Job 42:17) without saving another's soul. Thus, he, as well as all of mankind, have gone astray and have sinned (Psalm 14:1-3; 53:1-3; Ecclesiastes 7:20; Romans 3:10).

Satan would not have known, during his persecution of Job, whether Job had sinned in his heart because he cannot discern the thoughts and intents of the hearts of men; only God can do that. Satan told God that Job would fail the tests by cursing God to His face, suggesting an oral act. Job never did that. However, not one soul was saved as a result of Job's ultimate death. When Satan observed God's chastisement of Job and the death of Job, he undoubtedly believed that Job must have sinned in his heart as a result of the intense suffering he had to endure. This realization may have led Satan to further believe that, given enough suffering, every man will sin, at the least in his heart, and should he do so, he will suffer death for that sin just as surely as if he had sinned overtly. Satan clearly understood that, once any man sinned, his death would be for his own sin and therefore could not be for the sins of anyone else.

From his experience with Job, Satan mistakenly concluded that no man could endure the degree of suffering that he can put upon him and never sin overtly or in his heart. The Bible gives us a glimpse of the extent of the suffering Satan put upon Job. His oxen, asses, and camels were stolen from him (Job 1:14-15,17); his servants were killed (Job 1:15-17); his sheep were burned by a fire from heaven (Job 1:16); his seven sons and three daughters were killed when the home of one of them collapsed (Job 1:19); he was smitten with sore boils from head to foot (Job 2:7); he was the greatest of all the men of the east (Job 1:3) and received much respect (Job 29:7-25), but was left so poor that he resided among the ashes (Job 2:8); his flesh was caked with worms and clods of dust; his skin was cracked and broke out afresh (Job 7:5); he suffered terrible dreams and visions (Job 7:14); he was mocked by his friends (Job 12:4, 16:20); he wept unto God (Job 16:16,20); he saw his condition as hopeless (Job 19:10); all of his family and friends abandoned him (Job 19:13-19); his wife was repulsed by his breath (Job 19:17); he was literally skin and bones (Job 19:20); he enjoyed a personal relationship with God but felt abandoned (Job 23:8-17, 29:2-5); his bones gave him piercing pain at night and he suffered constant gnawing pain (Job 30:17) and his skin turned black and fell off of him and his bones burned with fever (Job 30:30).

Upon Job's successful completion of the tests by not overtly cursing God, God blessed Job with more than he had before the tests. Job did eventually die, and the Scriptures are silent as to whether Job sinned at any time after the tests.

Satan took this knowledge into his experience with Jesus. Satan had to know that Job was all man, with his attendant sin nature as a descendant of Adam; whereas Jesus had a human mother but God as His Father. Jesus therefore had both man's sinful nature and God's sinless nature. Satan also knew that Adam did not have a sin nature, and yet Satan was able to induce him to overtly sin against God. Satan was willing to put his own condemnation to the test in the hope that Jesus would also sin if the suffering was great enough.

Satan's persecutions of Job and Jesus would not have been possible unless God removed His hedge of protection from around them (Job 1:10; 2:4-6; Luke 22:53; John 7:30; 8:20). Satan was not allowed to kill Job. Jesus allowed Satan to take his life knowing that Satan's actions were according to the will of God, His Father. Satan left nothing untried in his bag of tricks when it came to his attempt to cause Jesus to sin as a result of his persecution unto death. He subjected Jesus to a degree of suffering worst than anything Job experienced. In fact, it was more suffering than any man will ever live to endure. In Isaiah 52:14, it is written:

> As many were astonished at thee; his visage was so marred more than any man, and his form more than the sons of men.

This verse tells us that the beatings and scourging that Jesus suffered at the hands of Satan, through sinful man, was worse than any human being will ever have to endure. The New Living Translation of Isaiah 52:14 is as follows:

> Many were amazed when they saw him—beaten and bloodied, so disfigured one would scarcely know he was a person.

This verse tells us that Jesus' disfigurement was so horrible that it was barely possible to tell that He was a human being. It is one thing for Jesus not to be recognized as Jesus because of the beatings, but this was far worse. He could barely be recognized as a person. Jesus underwent torture so extreme that no man will ever be called upon to suffer similar or greater suffering. Satan put Jesus through a degree of physical, emotional, and spiritual suffering that has never been nor ever will be experienced by mankind.

Jesus was fully aware of the degree and extent of suffering He was to endure for our sakes. In Matthew 26, Jesus prayed three times to His Father that, if it be His will, this cup be passed from Him. According to Luke 22:44, He agonized over His impending persecution so much so that His "sweat was as it were great drops of blood falling down to the ground."

It is important that we fully grasp the true nature and extent of Jesus' suffering for our sakes. It is extremely unfortunate that practically every depiction of the persecution and suffering Jesus lovingly endured fails to accurately reflect the totality of its gruesome details. Perhaps if we saw His suffering as it truly was, we would have a far greater appreciation for the tremendous price

God had to pay for the salvation of our souls, and the limitless love He has for every one of us.

Satan's insatiable desire to put unconscionable pain upon Jesus, the human manifestation of God, in an effort to cause Him to sin, blinded Satan from the repercussions of his actions. Job received twice as much as he possessed before the tests, and Jesus brought about the salvation of the world. It is ironic that the father of deception, through his experience with Job, deceived himself into performing the very acts upon the Son of God, which undid the consequences of Satan's initial deception of Adam and Eve. Praise be to God because Jesus, despite the horrific scourging, remained sinless to the end. Every child of God should be constantly praising, thanking and glorifying our God Who caused Satan to use his own deceptive nature against himself to the end that Jesus would be in a position to suffer and die for such undeserving creatures as us.

The Atoning Power of Jesus' Ultimate Sacrifice

Since death can only occur by the commission of sin, a sinless man will never know death. The death of such a man could pay the penalties of condemned souls. The Bible cites an incidence when the life of a sinless person was about to be offered, in part, for the sins of men. It is found in Genesis 22:1-19. This is, of course, the account of God's request that Isaac, the supernaturally born son of Abraham and Sarah, be offered as a sacrifice to God at, or near, the location where the supernaturally born Jesus would later be slain for the sins of the world (Genesis 22:2) and where Solomon built his holy temple (2 Chronicles 3:1).

God halted the sacrifice of Isaac at the last minute

and provided a ram in his stead (Genesis 22:13). The ram was used in Old Testament times for consecration (Exodus 29:22, 27, 31; Leviticus 8:22, 29), for atonement as a trespass offering (Leviticus 5:16-18; Numbers 5:8), and for a peace offering (Leviticus 9:4, 18; Numbers 6:14-17). Since this was the animal sacrificed in Isaac's stead, it is reasonable to conclude that Isaac was to be offered for the same reasons as the ram; namely, (1) to consecrate the place where Jesus would later give His life for the sins of the world and where the house of God was later to be built, (2) to temporarily atone for the sins of Abraham and his people, and (3) to serve as a peace offering to confirm their relationship with God.

We know that anything sacrificed unto God had to be free of any blemish (Deuteronomy 15:21). Indeed, each of the above-referenced passages concerning the sacrifice of a ram required the ram to be without blemish. Thus we can infer that there was no sin in Isaac as of the time he was to be offered as a sacrifice, and Abraham had to be aware of this fact. If so, Abraham knew that Isaac could not suffer death at that point in his life, even if Isaac was sacrificed. Clearly, Abraham expected Isaac to be resurrected (Hebrews 11:17-19).

God wanted to see if Abraham was willing to demonstrate his uncompromising and unconditional love for God by obediently sacrificing his son, Issac. God blessed Abraham for his willingness to obey God to this extent.

The nature and extent of his relationship with God would suggest that Abraham understood all too well the importance of what he was asked to do. The Holy Scriptures state that Abraham saw the redemption of man through Jesus Christ and was glad (John 8:56). Ultimately, Abraham and God offered their offspring to be sacrificed for the sins of the world because Jesus is Abraham's descendant (Luke 3:23-38) and the Son of God (John 3:16).

Jesus is a sinless progenitor, Who can give eternal life. The atoning power contained in Jesus' sinless, Godly blood, which was shed for the sins of mankind, was more than sufficient to pay the death penalties for all the sins of the world.

The Scriptures tell us that Jesus is the Way, the Truth, and the Life (John 14:6); that eternal life is in Him (John 1:4; 1 John 5:11); and that He is the Bread of Life (John 6:35, 48) Whose words are Spirit and Life (John 6:63). The life discussed in these scriptural passages is spiritual and eternal. However, Jesus knew that the life of the flesh is in the blood (Leviticus 17:11, 14). In order for us to be redeemed, the eternal life-filled blood of the Son of man, which is powerful enough to permanently cover the sins of every descendant of Adam and Eve, must be shed unto death.

Death is the absence of life, separation from God, and the wages of sin. As a result of Jesus' sinless sacrifice, death would have no victory over God's chosen people. The eternal life-giving power contained in every drop of Jesus' blood was extracted from His body in the most excruciating fashion. He was pierced through, utterly crushed and beaten with blows that cut in (Isaiah 53:5). His beard was literally plucked out of His cheeks (Isaiah 50:6). The Holy Scriptures also tell us of the extent of the power unleashed by the atoning death of Jesus, by describing the resurrection of the bodies of saints immediately upon Jesus' death. They went into Jerusalem and appeared unto many (Matthew 27:52-53). Upon His resurrection, all authority that is in heaven and earth was given to Jesus (Matthew 28:18).

No other creature in or under heaven could pay the death penalty for sinful man. We had to die for our sins. By one man's offense and disobedience all men became sinners and were condemned; but by the righteousness and obedience of Jesus Christ, the only begotten Son of God, many will be made righteous and justified (Romans 5:17-19; 1 John 4:9). The sacrificial shedding of the innocent, life-filled blood of God, through Jesus Christ, paid the physical and spiritual death penalties of all those who are willing to accept, in faith, this sacrifice on their behalf. Jesus' resurrection unto eternal life ensures that all of God's spiritually born offspring will be similarly resurrected and will never know eternal death. They shall be resurrected unto eternal life, just like Jesus, because their eternal physical and spiritual death penalties have been paid.

We have redemption through the shedding unto death of the life-filled blood of Jesus Christ, Who is the image of the invisible God (Colossians 1:14-15). By accepting God's sacrifice, through faith, for the forgiveness of our sins (Romans 3:25), we are indeed forgiven and receive an inheritance among the sanctified by faith, which is in Jesus Christ (Acts 26:18). "Inherit" means that it will be our birthright as the children of God to be His heirs and to possess all of the rights and privileges of being one with our Father. It is the power of our faith in Christ Jesus that brings about our salvation. By this faith we are spiritually begotten of God with the word of truth (James 1:18). We are God's creation in Jesus Christ unto good works (Ephesians 2:10), and we keep ourselves unspotted from this world (1 John 5:18-19).

We then put on the "new man, which after God is created" (Ephesians 4:23-24). This new man is spiritual and bears the image of the heavenly (1 Corinthians 11:7; 15:42-49; 2 Corinthians 3:18; Colossians 3:10). From then on, the Holy Spirit dwells in us and we become the temples of God (1 Corinthians 3:17; 6:19). We now have received the Spirit of God, and we speak spiritual words He teaches us (1 Corinthians 2:12-14). As the redeemed of the Lord, we are heirs of all the promises of God. We are His children, and He is our God and Father (Romans 8:15). We dwell in Him and He in us. Upon our glorification, we will be one with Him to the same extent as Jesus is one with God. In order for us to fully appreciate all that is meant by being one with God, we have to let the law of the Spirit of Life completely fill us with its righteousness (Romans 8:1-17). The Holy Spirit will take over our lives, influencing us to obey God and to do good works (2 Corinthians 10:5-6; 1 Peter 1:2).

There is a tendency for some of the lost or the less mature children of God to be apprehensive about the prospect of being filled with the Holy Spirit to the extent that He influences them to obey God and to do good works. They envision being possessed to the point that God takes over their bodies and they are relegated to a shell-like existence, while God takes away their free will.

In reality, we never lose control over our bodies or our lives. Instead, not only do we keep both, but we do so unto eternity, for it is written:

> He that loveth his life shall lose it; and he that hateth his life in this world shall keep it unto life eternal. (John 12:25)

When we are filled with the Holy Spirit, our sin
natures are replaced with God's nature. Even though our
carnal natures cause us to sin even if we do not want to
(Romans 7:13-22), our Spirit-filled natures cause us to
obey because we want to. If we give up our quest to be
separate but equal to God, we gain oneness with God
without losing our individuality. We get to experience
God from a first-person perspective, and we get to
collectively experience God with every other child of
God. When we become the children of God and joint
heirs of God with Jesus, we shall be glorified together
with Jesus (Romans 8:17) and become man in God and
God in man, just like Jesus.

We shall see in the next chapter that we, as members
of the Body of Christ, will have to individually and
collectively suffer to the same extent as Jesus suffered
(1 Peter 2:21). Just as Jesus was raised from the dead by
the Spirit of God, so shall the members of the Body of
Christ be raised from our physical and spiritual deaths
by the Spirit Who dwells in us (Romans 6:4; 8:11).

We have an opportunity, through Jesus, to
demonstrate our unconditional and uncompromising
love for our Creator God through obedience. Are you
willing to make good use of this benevolent
opportunity? With what is at stake, can we afford to
disregard it?

CHAPTER FIVE

OUR SPIRITUAL REBIRTHS AS THE CHILDREN OF GOD

God cannot become one with us unless His and our characteristics, attributes and mannerisms are compatible. This type of compatibility is best demonstrated through the person of Jesus Christ. In this chapter, we shall discuss why every reborn child of God will take on the image of Jesus as it relates to His personality traits. We shall compare these traits with those of the unsaved whose characteristics resemble and therefore are compatible with those of Satan. We shall discuss how the life, death and resurrection of Jesus Christ provide us with the means to claim victory over death and to be adopted as sons and daughters of God. Each child of God is reborn with a measure of spiritual gifts as determined by the will of God. Finally, we shall delve into the Holy Scriptures to better understand the requirement that every member of the Body of Christ must suffer just as Jesus suffered to an extent and degree as, again, determined by the Holy will of God.

The Reborn Children of God

As we have repeatedly stated, when Adam and Eve were first created, they were created in the image and after the likeness of God. Upon their fall from grace, all of their descendants were born in their image and after their likeness. Jesus was called upon to pay the ultimate price for the redemption of Adam and Eve and their progeny. Thus anyone who accepts Jesus' sacrifice for the remission of his sins, in faith, will be restored to the original position of Adam and Eve, in the image and after the likeness of God, as a child of God. God confirms this glorious fact on numerous occasions throughout the Holy Scriptures. Colossians 3:10 and 1 John 3:2 tell us that we have become new individuals renewed in knowledge after the image of Him that created us.

John 4:24 tells us that God is a Spirit and we who worship Him must worship Him in spirit. In order to do this, we must become the children of God by being spiritually reborn in Christ Jesus. James 1:18 tells us that God begot us with the word of truth (i.e., Jesus Christ) to be a kind of firstfruits of His creatures. This verse appears to make an analogy to the Old Testament tithing of firstfruits found in the book of Genesis. In other words, the reborn children of God are the first form of offering to God in the redemptive process of all creation. When this occurs, 2 Corinthians 5:17 tells us that we become new creatures, that old things are passed away and all things are become new. Ephesians 4:23-24 tell us that we will then be renewed in the spirit of our mind. We will put on the "new man, which after God is created in righteousness and true holiness."

God, who foreknew all of His chosen children prior

to their earthly existence, predestined us to be conformed to the image of His Son, which is His image (Jeremiah 1:5; Romans 8:29). Philippians 1:6 tells us that He who began a good work in us will complete it. As we grow spiritually, our spiritual Father, Who loves us beyond measure, will correct us and chasten us just as our earthly fathers do (Hebrews 12:3-11). We walk in the Spirit (Galatians 5:16) and indeed are led by the Spirit (Galatians 5:18). As we have discussed, our Father is Spirit and He dwells in our reborn spirits. Anyone who is reborn of God cannot habitually sin because God's seed is in him (1 John 3:9; 5:18-19). Through our Father's guidance, we shall develop into mature, spiritual children, and His faithfulness will cause us to realize the perfect oneness that was the originally intended relationship between the Creator and His highest creation.

Through the Holy Scriptures, God reveals to us the purposes behind the creation of the spiritual and physical realms. The Holy Spirit enlightens the spiritually reborn children of God about the nature, attributes and characteristics of our triune Godhead by opening our spiritual eyes to who we are and why we were created. Unless we are spiritually born again, we will not see these things. We will see and hear physically but not spiritually. You see, our spiritual senses are and will continue to be dead. We will be oblivious to God's master plan for us that was established before the foundation of the world. Without this rebirth and spiritual sense of direction, we are truly lost.

Salvation is achieved when, as lost persons, we repent of our sins and accept the sacrifice of Jesus

Christ for the propitiation of our sins and welcome Him into our hearts as our Lord and Savior. Salvation is a free gift and is not based on good works. Therefore no one can boast that he earned his salvation. When we come to that point in our lives where we realize that it is our nature to sin and that we cannot save ourselves from the consequences of our sins in this life or the next, we desperately cry out for salvation. We then become mindful of God's promise that we will be saved if we believe, in faith, that He sent His only begotten Son to die for all the sins of mankind.

I reached this turning point in my life midway through evening law school in 1984. I was dating an evening law student from another law school when we became aware that she was pregnant. I was a bachelor, and she was a single parent of one child. Neither of us had an intimate, close and personal relationship with the Lord. We agonized over whether we should raise the child or have an abortion, but it seemed to me that the focus was on our professional careers instead of the life of the unborn child. Ultimately, we both agreed that an abortion would be in our best interests. If we considered the interests of the unborn child at all, it was of minor significance when compared to our interests. At least from my perspective, the same could be said of any consideration I may have given with respect to God's interests concerning the life of the unborn child.

Our relationship ended shortly thereafter. I am convinced that the abortion had something to do with our parting of the ways. I thought that this would have enabled me to have a fresh start, but it was only the beginning of my sorrows.

I was always somewhat fearless, to the extent that I

tried to meet all challenges head-on, regardless of the consequences, especially if I thought I was right. The problem was that I could not convince myself that the abortion was right. In fact, I became increasingly convinced that I had committed a great wrong. This was not something that I was going to be able to shrug off. It nagged at me at every turn. It was affecting my schoolwork, my employment and my every waking hour. I could find no rest or comfort. I knew that I could not bring back the life of this innocent child. I felt as if all was lost. I did not believe that any amount of success or fortune could erase the overwhelming sense of hopelessness and guilt that had taken over my life. I was not able to bury myself in my schoolwork or day job to rid myself of the shame and guilt.

I knew from my upbringing of an option that promised to remove all of my burdens, including this most heavy one. That option is Jesus. My situation was dire. I recalled Jesus' promise that He would take on our burdens and forgive us our sins. I had to personally go before my Lord and Savior and put my faith in His promises on the line. I had to confess my sins and seek His forgiveness. If I was going to give all that I am to Jesus, I had to have a face-to-face, heart-to-heart talk with Him. I could then tell Him how much of a mess I have made with my life and that I am totally relying on Him to keep His promises to forgive me unto salvation; to take on my burdens and to live in and through me from then on.

So, in deep contrition, I got on my knees and asked Jesus into my life. Now that I was giving myself over to Him, it had to be 100 percent. My every breath, step and thought would be under His control for the rest of my

life. I understood that this would be a gradual spiritual
growth process but my submission at that moment was
total and complete. I gave my life to Christ and was
spiritually reborn. As I stood up, I felt a tremendous
feeling of relief and freedom. It's the kind of feeling one
gets when he knows that everything is going to be all
right even though there is no earthly reason to feel that
way. I continued to experience this same inner peace
and joy every time I subsequently turned my burdens
over to the Lord. I was convinced that all of my sins
were forgiven and that Jesus had accepted my invitation
to come into my life. It was now His life to be lived
through me, and I welcomed Him.

Just as we were babes when we were physically
born, we are also babes when we are spiritually reborn.
Thus we start out with spiritual milk (1 Corinthians 3:1-
2). As we mature as Christians, we can have spiritual
meat as well as drink (1 Corinthians 10:3-4). What is
this spiritual milk and spiritual meat? It is none other
than the Word of God: Jesus Christ. On several
occasions in the Holy Scriptures, it talks about "tasting
the Lord." Deuteronomy 8:3 and Matthew 4:4 tell us
that man lives not by bread alone, but by every word
that proceeds out of the mouth of God. Since Jesus is
the literal word of God, He is the Bread of Life. The
verb "proceeds" is in the present tense, denoting an
ongoing process. Psalm 34:8 tells us to taste and see that
the Lord is good. This can only be done spiritually (1
Peter 2:1-5). As we are spiritually fed the living Word
of God, we are ultimately filled with the Holy Spirit
(Ephesians 5:18-21). We are, then, not in the flesh but in
the Spirit, and the Spirit in us (Romans 8:8-10).

Jesus said, "I am the resurrection, and the life: he

that believeth in me, though he were dead, yet shall he live" (John 11:25). John 1:4 says about Jesus: "In him was life; and the life was the light of men." These passages imply that Jesus, being the every utterance of God, can only speak that which is of God, namely spirit and life. These verses also say that the Word of God is pleasing to the spiritual taste buds. When we spiritually eat the Word of God, we spiritually live.

In John 6:22-58, Jesus discusses the spiritually reborn child's need for spiritual nourishment. Jesus, teaching the people at Capernaum, explained to them that they should not seek after Him because He feeds them physical food, but that they should seek after Him for the food that never perishes and lasts forever so that one hungers no more. But in order to do so, they must believe on Him whom God hath sent. Jesus goes on to explain that He is the Bread of Life; no man can come to Him unless the Father draws him.

By spiritually eating and drinking the Word of God, we can have eternal life. Everyone who gains this eternal life must spiritually eat the flesh of the Son of Man and spiritually drink His blood (John 6:53). Obviously, Jesus was not discussing the eating or drinking of His physical flesh and blood. Jesus is the Word of God, and so he who reads or hears the Word of God spiritually eats and drinks of it and will have everlasting life.

We have talked about spiritually tasting the good Word of God, but what about tasting the powers of the age to come? These powers are those of our triune Godhead that will be exercised in and through us during the millennium age and forevermore when we are spiritually glorified. It is only then that God will have completed His good work in us to do His will (Philippians 1:6; Hebrews 12:23; 13:20-21). We cannot begin to imagine what it will be like to be active participants as God demonstrates His awesome power over all of creation in and through us for all eternity. When this happens to a child of God, he will no longer utter deceit (Job 27:3-4) and he will possess each of the characteristics of Jesus, the head of the spiritual Body of Christ.

The Characteristics of the Children of God

In Matthew 5:3-12, Jesus describes, through the Beatitudes, what the personality traits are of every reborn child of God. We do not possess one or some of these traits. We possess all of them, just as Jesus does. Once spiritually reborn, we are transformed into the image of Jesus. We resemble Him in appearance but, more importantly, we resemble Him in His ways and characteristics. We are poor in spirit; mourners; meek; hungry and thirsty for righteousness; merciful; pure in heart; peacemakers; and persecuted for righteousness' and for Jesus' sake. As possessors of these personality traits, we shall receive all of the blessings that are set forth in these verses. We shall therefore inherit the kingdom of heaven; be comforted; inherit the earth; be completely satisfied; obtain mercy; see God; and receive a great reward in heaven. These traits and resultant blessings go hand-in-hand. They are mutually inclusive.

As the children of God spiritually nurtured with the Word of God, we begin to bear the fruit of the Spirit and manifest love, joy, peace, longsuffering, gentleness, goodness, faith, meekness, temperance, tender mercies, humbleness, forbearance and charity (Galatians 5:22-26;

Colossians 3:12-17). It will become more and more difficult for us to sin. We will still sin, but we will sin less and less and less. For it is written, he who is born of God cannot sin (1 John 3:9). God is telling us in this verse that we will not give in to habitual sin.

How wonderful it will be to live in God's kingdom, which will be composed only of citizens who, being one with God, will exhibit these Godly characteristics. Imagine, if you will, millions, if not billions, of people who resemble Jesus in every way. The creative energy and power of only one of these faithful children of God would be too great to fathom, let alone billions of people who can do all that Jesus did in His earthly ministry and more. The traffic of supernatural events destined to simultaneously take place in every corner of the universe, involving dimensions as of yet unknown, is simply too mind-boggling for us to appreciate. Even more exciting is the fact that all of this will be accomplished by the humblest of people, each of whom in-dwells God and God in-dwells them being individually and collectively one with Him. They will be all-knowing, all-powerful and ever-present and will have as their very natures all of God's characteristics, attributes and mannerisms including His unconditional, uncompromising, limitless and selfless love. We live in the hope of this eventuality but our timeless eternal God is experiencing it now.

The Characteristics of the Children of Satan

Just as the children of God possess the personality traits of Jesus, the children of disobedience possess the personality traits of their father, the devil. They are liars; participators in unnatural sex; filled with all unrighteousness, fornication, wickedness, covetousness, maliciousness, envy, murder, strife, deceit, evil-mindedness; whisperers; backbiters; haters of God; violent; proud; boasters; inventors of evil things; disobedient to parents; without understanding; covenant breakers; without natural affection; unforgiving; and unmerciful (Romans 1:21-31). They not only do all these terrible things but they also take pleasure in anyone who does these things (Romans 1:32).

When Satan became one with man through sin, Satan's sinful nature became man's sinful nature. The children of Satan sin because the devil has sinned from the beginning (1 John 3:8). Being carnally minded, they are enemies of God and cannot be subjected to His law (Romans 8:7). The children of God are spiritually fed the bread and wine of God, which is the metaphorical body and blood of Jesus Christ. The children of Satan spiritually eat the bread of wickedness and drink the wine of violence (Proverbs 4:17). They do the lusts of their father, the devil (John 8:44).

Adam and Eve may not have fully understood the extent of their relationship with Satan that was established as a result of their sin. They thought that they could be their own boss, that they could give birth to a people and provide for their physical and spiritual needs forever without any assistance from God or Satan. In reality, they are either God's children destined for eternal life and oneness with Him or Satan's children destined for eternal damnation, destruction and oneness with him. It must be one or the other. Neutrality is not an option. Jesus said that He will vomit out of His mouth all who are lukewarm (Revelations 3:15-16).

Being lukewarm in our obedience to the Lord is

probably something that every one of us has had to deal with in one form or fashion, especially in these times when tolerance and compromise is the order of the day. As spiritually reborn children of God, we must love God with all our hearts, souls and minds.

In the end, we all are either extremists for God or for Satan. We either love God with all of our hearts, souls and minds or we love Satan and the world to this extent. All those in the middle are treated by Christ worst than those who are extremists for Satan. We should draw comfort and strength in the knowledge that we are considered extremists for God. If this is to be our walk with God, then let all the people of God say Amen. Unfortunately, many will shy away from this walk with God.

It is written:

> Enter ye in at the strait gate: for wide is the gate, and broad is the way, that leadeth to destruction, and many there be which go in there at:
> Because strait is the gate, and narrow is the way, which leadeth unto life, and few there be that find it (Matthew 7:13-14).

In the Garden of Eden, Adam, being tempted with the lust of his flesh, the lust of his eyes, and the pride of life, could have chosen to eat from the Tree of Life and not of the Tree of the Knowledge of Good and Evil. Had he done so, he would have attained eternal life in an incorruptible body. We are daily confronted with the same choice Adam had. We can either choose to spiritually eat the Word of God and have eternal life, or we can choose to spiritually eat Satan's words and have eternal damnation with him. There is no middle ground. Our hearts will determine the choices we make.

Our Victory Over Satan Through Jesus Christ

In Revelation 22:19, the world is warned not to take away from the words of that book lest God take away their part out of the Book of Life, the Holy City, and from the things which are written in that prophetic book. This warning would appear to apply as well to all inspired scripture which is the Word of God (Deuteronomy 4:2; Proverbs 30:6; Galatians 1:6-7). Almost all Greek manuscripts concerning this passage in Revelation 22 read "tree of life" instead of "book of life." Both of these phrases refer to Jesus, who is "the life" (John 11:25).

Jesus, therefore, is the Tree of Life, the Book of Life, the Holy Scriptures and, indeed, life itself. Jesus is the only source of eternal life. He came that we may have life and have it more abundantly (John 10:10). When He abides in us and we in Him, we have a degree of living that is eternal and far superior than anything we may temporarily enjoy without Him. Until we accept Him as our Lord and Savior, we are not a part of Jesus. He does not abide in us and we truly are lifeless. How wondrous is the second personage of our triune Godhead!

In order for us to get to this state of completeness in and through Jesus, we must be able to stand against "the wiles of the devil" (Ephesians 6:11), who comes "to steal, and to kill, and to destroy" (John 10:10). This is spiritual hand-to-hand combat, the outcome of which determines the future of our souls. This battle does not occur against men.

> For we wrestle not against flesh and blood, but
> against principalities, against powers, against the
> rulers of the darkness of this world, against
> spiritual wickedness in high places. (Ephesians
> 6:12)

But take heart; this is a war that we cannot lose. For "if God be for us, who can be against us?" (Romans 8:31). As victors, we are given eternal life that cannot be taken away from us (John 10:28-30; 17:2; Romans 2:7; 1 John 2:25).

In 2 Corinthians 12:1-10, the apostle Paul relates to us that he was given "a thorn in the flesh" which he defines as a messenger of Satan to beat him. I interpret this phrase to mean something physical which occasionally caused him to sin. He tells us that he asked God to remove this thing from him on three occasions but God told him that His grace is sufficient for him. In other words, no matter how many times we lose the ongoing battle with our sin natures, His grace is ever present to forgive us. Through our weakness, He demonstrates His strength. After all, it is not our ability to remain sinless that secures our salvation. That was secured by Jesus Christ while we were yet sinners (Romans 5:8). It is our ever-developing intimacy with God which makes it easier for us to resist our sin natures, but there will still be occasions when our sinful natures win out. In every instance, God's grace is there to forgive us allowing us to maintain the same degree of intimacy with God which we enjoyed before each sin.

While this war is fought on an individual soul-by-soul basis, it is also fought collectively by the entire Body of Christ, of which we are members (1 Corinthians 12:12-14). The Holy Scriptures tell us that

the spiritually reborn children of God compose the Body
of Christ. They are silent, however, as to when the
spiritual Body of Christ will be complete. Though
unknown, it is believed by some that Jesus' return will
coincide with the completion of His spiritual Body
when the last soul has been saved.

Each of us is an individual member of that Body
(Ephesians 5:30-31), with Jesus Christ as the Head.
(Colossians 1:18). Just as every member of the physical
body has an individual function, every member of the
Body of Christ also has an individual purpose which
must be performed in order for the overall function of
the Body to be perfect (Ephesians 4:11-16). The
Scriptures describe these individual functions as
spiritual gifts, which each member of the Body of Christ
must identify and then exercise (Romans 12:4-8; 1
Corinthians 12:1-31).

The Spiritual Gifts of the Children of God

The moment we by faith accept God's promise of
salvation and turn our lives over to Christ, we are
spiritually born of God. We are physically born of man
but spiritually born of God just like Jesus. The Holy
Scriptures refer to every spiritually reborn person as the
child of God. As such, we are destined to be heirs to all
that is God's and, upon maturity and glorification, will
co-exist and be completely one with God. One day we
will be given incorruptible bodies and will be both the
physical and spiritual children of God. This means that
our bodies shall never again be susceptible to death,
illness, deterioration, or evil. We shall be immortal and
Godly in every respect. Until that day, as the spiritually
born children of God, the Spirit of God lives in us and is

a part of us. As we grow spiritually, we begin to identify and develop the spiritual gifts bestowed upon us by the Holy Spirit at our spiritual births. Our joy comes in the exercising of our spiritual gifts to the glory and honor of our Father, and the fulfillment of His will.

Thus, we are encouraged to follow after charity and desire spiritual gifts because, once we identify and develop them, we can perform our necessary functions in the Body of Christ (1 Corinthians 14:1). Every child of God is able to minister his unique gifts one to another, as good stewards of the manifold grace of God (1 Peter 4:10-11).

As spiritually reborn children of God, it is essential that we begin to understand and, indeed, use our spiritual gifts. Paul tells us in 1 Corinthians 12:4-11 that there are diversities of gifts, administrations and operations, but the same Spirit, Lord and God, which works all in all. In these passages, Paul lists some of the spiritual gifts that are given by the Holy Spirit. They are wisdom; the word of knowledge; faith; healing; the working of miracles; prophecy; discerning of spirits; divers kinds of tongues and interpretation of tongues. In Romans 12:3-8, these gifts are further identified to include ministry, teaching, exhortation, giving and ruling. The Holy Spirit gives these spiritual gifts to every child of God severally as He will. We are cautioned, however, to try the spirits to ensure that everyone who claims to be ministering spiritual gifts is indeed doing so (1 John 4:1-6). We are counseled to put on the whole armor of God to ward off evil spirits with evil intentions (Ephesians 6:10-18).

The extent to which we are able to use our spiritual gifts is directly dependent upon the extent of our spiritual growth. Our spiritual growth is measured by the extent of our faith. The degree to which we are spiritually mature is directly related to the extent to which we can, through faith, access the limitless power of God. That is why the Holy Spirit tells us in James 5:14 to call on the elders of the church to pray over and anoint with oil the sick in the name of the Lord.

It is unfortunate that it takes the children of God so many years to grow enough in faith so that the Holy Spirit, who indwells them, can manifest His power through them as the spiritual gift of healing. It takes us so long to recognize and effectively utilize our God-given gifts because we allow our sin natures to hold us back. We have been set free from this sin-nature bondage, but we must live in that freedom in order for the Holy Spirit to powerfully and yet lovingly manifest Himself in and through us by way of our spiritual gifts. It is only then that we will begin to bear spiritual fruit and enjoy the benefits of being a child of God.

The Requirement of Suffering for the Children of God

We who were chosen by God to be His children compose the spiritual Body of Christ. It is important that we understand what the Spirit of God is telling us when He refers to all children of God as composing the Body of Christ. Just like Aaron and his descendants in the Old Testament served as a priesthood to God for the people of Israel, Jesus and the spiritually reborn of God are a generation chosen to be a royal priesthood (1 Peter 2:9) making supplications, prayers, intercessions and thanks on behalf of all mankind (1 Timothy 2:1). As a holy priesthood, we offer up spiritual sacrifices acceptable to

God (1 Peter 2:4-5). We, who are the express image of Jesus, being members of His Body, are made to be kings and priests (Revelation 1:6; 5:10). We acquire our royalty and priestly status through Christ Jesus who is King of Kings (Revelation 17:14) and the high priest (Hebrews 7:11-28).

The Holy Scriptures often refer to every member of the Body of Christ as a saint (Romans 1:7; 1 Corinthians 1-2; 6:1-2; 2 Corinthians 1:1; Ephesians 1:1; Philippians 1:1; Colossians 1:2; Philemon 1:5) who will reign with Christ Jesus, being the King of saints (Revelation 15:3). Becoming a king and priest is a high calling that every child of God should desire to attain. The Apostle Paul writes in Philippians 3:14: "I press toward the mark for the prize of the high calling of God in Christ Jesus."

But just as Jesus physically and spiritually suffered in this world, every member of His spiritual Body must do likewise, according to his or her purpose and place in the Body as determined by the will of God. The faithfulness of God will preserve our souls so that our suffering will not be in vain. It is the same faithfulness of God that ensures that Christ's suffering can never be in vain. We cannot be members of Jesus Christ's body if we do not suffer as He suffered. Every part of His body suffered for our sins. After Jesus' resurrection, while in His glorified body, He appeared to His disciples, including Thomas, still bearing all of his sacrificial wounds (John 20:27-29). Revelation 5:6, as well as other passages of the Bible, describe the Lamb "as it had been slain" before the throne of God during the tribulation. Jesus, who is that Lamb of God, continues to bear the wounds of His sacrifice at least until God's redemptive plan has been completed.

There is no other option for the children of God. For He tells us in 2 Timothy 3:12 that all who will live Godly in Jesus Christ shall suffer persecution. He did not say that some will suffer; He said all will suffer persecution.

Therefore Romans 12:1-2 tells us to

> present your bodies a living sacrifice, holy, acceptable unto God, which is your reasonable service. And be not conformed to this world: but be ye transformed by the renewing of your mind, that ye may prove what is that good, and acceptable, and perfect, will of God.

What is this suffering that we are expected to endure? According to Mark 10:21, we may be called upon to give up all worldly possessions. Deprivation of earthly possessions, whether self-induced or otherwise, is a form of suffering in a materialistic world. Jesus had no earthly wealth to speak of (2 Corinthians 8:9). It is only when we do not seek or value earthly possessions that our heavenly Father gives them to us. We are then able to put them in their proper perspective, knowing as we do that they are not our possessions at all; they are God's.

This is the lesson taught to us through the parable of the rich young ruler who obeyed God's commandments in every respect but was told by Jesus that he lacked one thing, and that was to sell all he had and to take up the cross and follow Him. The young man went away sad because he was not willing to suffer financially for Christ. He thought that his riches were his and not God's. He did not want to part with what he really did not own. He had stored up all of his hope and aspirations in earthly treasures. If he possessed the Godly characteristic of unconditional and uncompromising love, he would have willingly and gladly parted with the riches he possessed and followed Jesus, because he would have wanted to demonstrate his love of God by being obedient to Jesus thereby storing up eternal treasures in heaven.

Thus we are cautioned that it is extremely difficult and almost impossible for one, who believes that he owns the earthly riches he was blessed to possess, to enter into the Kingdom of Heaven (Mark 10:23-27). In chapter 6 of his first letter to Timothy, the apostle Paul explains why it is so hard for the rich to keep their heart with God and how, by putting their trust in God, they can simultaneously enjoy their God-given riches and their relationship with their Creator. It is not an evil thing to be blessed with riches. Abraham, Job, David, Solomon and other great men of God were so blessed. However, when we treasure our worldly possessions more than our intimacy with our heavenly Father, we demonstrate our lack of love for Him. "For where your treasure is, there will your heart be also" (Matthew 6:21).

Obviously, our suffering is also physical since we are to take up the cross and suffer just as Jesus physically suffered unto death for us. Indeed, God's children have suffered all manner of physical persecution since the death and resurrection of Jesus Christ. Such persecutions continue to this very day. If we suffer in the flesh for the glory of Christ, we are told that we cease from sin (1 Peter 4:1) and that we will fare better at our judgment before Christ (1 Peter 4:12-19).

Finally, our suffering is emotional because we shall suffer false accusations (Matthew 5:11) and tribulations

(Romans 5:3; 2 Thessalonians 1:4). Yet none of these trials can separate us from the love of Christ (Romans 8:35). Indeed, God uses all of our sufferings to perfect, establish and settle us (1 Peter 5:10). In 2 Corinthians 12:10, Paul writes:

> Therefore I take pleasure in infirmities, in reproaches, in necessities, in persecutions, in distresses for Christ's sake: for when I am weak, then am I strong.

The more we suffer for Christ's sake, the stronger we become because it is through our divine deliverance from these travails that we see the power of God manifested in our lives. The more intimate we become with Jesus through these trials and tribulations, the more we are able to see, understand and take on the characteristics and attributes of God which shall completely replace our sinful natures upon our spiritual rebirths, glorification and unification with God. Because we have suffered with Jesus, we shall be glorified with Him (Romans 8:17) and will reign with Him (2 Timothy 2:12).

Therefore we must believe on Jesus Christ and suffer for His sake (Philippians 1:29). It is better, if God wills it, that we suffer for good than for bad (1 Peter 3:17). Jesus Christ suffered leaving us an example that we should follow his steps (1 Peter 2:21). It may very well be that every reborn child of God, depending on where in the Body of Christ he or she is located, will suffer to the same extent that the corresponding part of the physical body of Jesus suffered.

Obviously, certain parts of Jesus' body bore the brunt of His persecution. However, since He was tortured to the point that He was barely recognizable as a person, very few parts of His body were spared the shedding of blood. Nonetheless, the Holy Spirit tells us that when one member of Jesus' body suffers, all the other members suffer (1 Corinthians 12:26). Once our Lord can say "It is finished" with respect to the suffering of His collective spiritual Body, the time for His, and our, glorious return to reign as one with Him forever may be but a command of God away. While Jesus knew when His earthly sacrifice would be finished (John 19:30), only God knows the day and hour when the sacrifice of the collective spiritual Body of Christ is finished and the Son of man will return (Mark 13:24-37).

This requirement of suffering further explains why the road to heaven is narrow with few on it and why the road to damnation is wide and many are on it. Few are willing to suffer materially, physically and emotionally for the glory of Jesus Christ even though our redemption was accomplished by the material, physical and emotional sacrifice of God Himself through Jesus Christ. Many are unwilling to demonstrate the same measure of love that God so passionately showed us.

As members of the Body of Christ, all who wish to accept this redemption must endure to the end the same sacrificial suffering, each according to the manner and prescription as determined by the will of God. We must be willing to give up our sin-nature and be transformed to His God-nature, which is our predestination. If we choose not to do so and remain unsaved, we will lose our lives. However, if we choose to give up our sinful lives and be transformed, we will live forever. Thus, in Matthew 10:39, Jesus tells us: "He that findeth his life shall lose it: and he that loseth his life for my sake shall find it."

For many Christians it is difficult to accept the teachings of Jesus that we are members of one body, His Body, and as such must suffer as He suffered (especially since that necessarily means that some of us may suffer more than others even though we may be members of undesirable and seemingly insignificant parts of the Body of Christ).

The best scriptural passage that explains the relationship between the different members of the Body of Christ is contained in Paul's first letter to the Corinthians. In 1 Corinthians 12 Paul states that, as the physical body is one and has many members, all being members of that one body, so is the Body of Christ. We are baptized by one Spirit into the Body of Christ, whether we are Jews or Gentiles, bond or free. We have all been made to drink into one Spirit. He goes on to explain that no member of the body can remove itself because it isn't as important as it would like to be, implying that some members of the Body of Christ may feel that their position and function in the Body is not commensurate with the degree of suffering they are asked to endure. God has set the members the way He would have them—as it pleases Him.

Our Functions as Members of the Body of Christ

Each member of the Body of Christ is assigned a function unique unto himself that must be identified and exercised so that the Body can be whole. In addition, each member of the Body has need of every other member (1 Corinthians 12:12-31). The apostle Paul informs us that we bestow on those members of the

Body that we think to be less honorable more abundant honor and comeliness. Jesus said: "He that is least among you all, the same shall be great" (Luke 9:48). When describing John the Baptist, Jesus said that, despite his greatness, the least in the Kingdom of Heaven shall be greater than John the Baptist (Matthew 11:11). In other words, no matter how great our functions may be on earth as members of the Body of Christ, it cannot compare to the least in the Kingdom of Heaven because the rewards there makes everything here pale in comparison.

This is how God has composed the Body of Christ, so that there would be no schism in the Body: the comely parts having no need of honor; but the uncomely parts, thought to be less honorable, needing and obtaining more abundant honor (1 Corinthians 12:23). In this way, the Body of Christ is whole, complete and perfect. If one member suffers, all suffer; if one member is honored, all are honored and rejoice (1 Corinthians 12:26).

Paul concludes by using the analogy of the physical body, saying that we are all the Body of Christ and yet members in particular, each having different functions with different gifts. In another letter Paul tells us that, ultimately, we should strive for love and not spiritual gifts or glorified functions of the Body (Romans 12:3-21). Given what we have discussed concerning the overriding importance of Godly love in God's ordered creation, we should have some measure of appreciation for and understanding about why the apostle Paul places so much emphasis on love.

God does not honor any one member of the Body of Christ more than any other. When Moses exhorted Israel to love the stranger and fear the Lord because of the great things He had done for them, he emphasized that God shows no partiality nor takes bribes (Deuteronomy 10:12-22). Jehoshaphat set up judges in the land of Judah and told them to fear the Lord when they judge because there is no iniquity with the Lord, nor does He respect people. Again, we are reminded that the Lord does not take bribes (2 Chronicles 19:4-7).

When Peter preached to the Gentiles, he told them that, of a truth, God is impartial (Acts 10:34). Paul said the same thing in his letter to the Romans (Romans 2:11) and in his letter to the Galatians (Galatians 2:6). Whether we are children of parents, servants, masters, bond or free, we are to perform our functions willingly as the servants of Christ, doing the will of God from the heart, "knowing that [our] Master also is in heaven; neither is there respect of persons with him" (Ephesians 6:1-9).

Just as God does not show partiality to anyone, Jesus also does not favor one part of His body over any other part. We are all equal partakers of the Bread of Life (1 Corinthians 10:17). An excellent illustration of the equality between the members of the Body of Christ is contained in the parable of the workers in the vineyard (Matthew 20:1-16). In this parable, Jesus describes the kingdom of heaven as being full of workers who, at the end of the day, are paid the same wages regardless of whether they worked the entire day, three quarters, half, one quarter, or the last hour of the day. Jesus reasoned that this is so because He is allowed to do as He wills with His own.

Jesus tells us that whenever someone comes to Him, being drawn by God, Jesus will in no way cast him out (John 6:37). In other words, once we are saved, we will always be saved. If this were not true, then the eternal life every child of God obtains by receiving the Spirit of God when spiritually reborn is not eternal at all, and the promises contained in John 3:15; 4:36; 10:28; and 17:2 are lies. John 10:28 and Ephesians 5:30 essentially say that one who has been given to Jesus by God receives eternal life; is sealed by the Holy Ghost until the day of redemption and cannot be plucked out of the hands of our triune Godhead.

As spiritually reborn members of the Body of Christ, we are one with Him and are no longer of this world, as He is not of this world. We are hated by this world just as He was hated. However, though we are hated and persecuted by the powers and principalities that temporarily control this world, we are loved by God. When we are fully restored to our original estate, having incorruptible and glorified bodies full of the eternal life-giving blood of Jesus, we will then be sufficiently compatible with God to be completely inhabited by Him, enabling Him to manifest Himself in and through us forever. As His holy temples, individually and collectively, we will become active participants with God as He lives and acts through and by us forevermore.

It is one thing to live in the faith that we shall one day be resurrected unto eternal life. It is yet another thing to know that we shall be resurrected in glory as children of Almighty God who are imbued with His mannerisms, attributes and characteristics and who will live in His holy name.

It is almost beyond belief that we shall be resurrected and glorified as one with our Father Creator; His Son, Jesus Christ; and the Holy Spirit in every good way imaginable and to live and reign with Them forever. Can there be any created purpose in or under heaven greater than this? Is this not worth our most loving obedience? Are you willing to give up all selfish desires to be like God and to suffer, to any extent required, in order to become one with Him? Are you willing to die to self so that you can live as one with God? The Holy Word of God loves us so much that He became one of us to show us exactly what it will be like to be one with God through loving obedience; and He suffered death so that we could realize His level of oneness with God as we were originally created to experience.

EPILOGUE

All that God created was initially perfect and good. Mankind is God's greatest creation, and we are the culmination of God's creative process. God made us in His image and after His likeness. The perfection of all of creation is dependent upon our perfection, which is itself dependent upon our compatibility with God in terms of appearance and attributes. According to God's holy will, Adam and Eve were given an opportunity to permanently secure this perfection for which they were created by becoming, through uncompromising, unconditional, loving obedience, one with their Creator. Permanent perfection is a prerequisite because God is perfect in all His ways.

From the moment of our creation, we resembled God in appearance and personality. The incorporation of the righteous and holy characteristics of God into every human being enabled us to be congruous physical temples of God. This compatibility with God makes it possible not only for God to inhabit us but also for us to inhabit God. For it is written in Ephesians 2:19-22:

> Now therefore ye are no more strangers and foreigners, but fellow citizens with the saints, and of the household of God; And are built upon the foundation of the apostles and prophets, Jesus Christ himself being the chief corner stone;
> In whom all the building fitly framed together groweth unto an holy temple in the Lord: In whom ye also are builded together for an habitation of God through the Spirit.

Our lives are intended to be mirror images of God's

life, so much so that the life of God becomes our lives. Praise be to God!

However, God wanted each of us to willingly choose to experience this oneness with Him not because of the awesome privileges and benefits attendant thereto, but because of a desire to obey the Word of God out of love, honor and respect. Just as a man and woman voluntarily pledge to love, honor and respect each other in a marriage ceremony, God requires every one of His children to make that kind of commitment to Him.

So God decided to test Adam and Eve to determine if they would choose God's way to eternal perfection through obedient love or their own way unto death through disobedient hatred. This test was conducted in the Garden of Eden, and it was very simple: obey Me and live, or disobey Me and die. In other words, demonstrate your God-given ability to love your Creator more than you love yourself through obedience, even if you believe that it is not in your interests to do so, and you will live. Otherwise, you will suffer death through eternal separation from God and damnation. God imbued both Adam and Eve with free will and did not tell them about the fullness of their reward, so that the extent of their love of God would be the determining factor in this test of obedience.

Satan, one of the greatest angelic beings created by God, albeit now fallen and the architect of all evil, understood God's creative process. He understood man's role in it and therefore the significance of the test. Satan wanted to be more than he was created to be. He wanted to be like God, and his prideful plan to overthrow God resulted in his ignominious fall. Satan knew that God intended to rule the heavens and the universe by becoming one with His greatest creation through love. Satan wanted to rule the heavens and the universe by becoming one with man through sin. He had to accomplish this before Adam and Eve ate from the Tree of Life and thereby perfect their oneness with God through loving obedience. Satan reasoned that it would be impossible for them to perfect their oneness with God should they sin.

Had God decided to become eternally one with Adam and Eve at the moment of their creation, then a test would not have been necessary and Satan would never have had an opportunity to attempt the usurpation of God's authority through mankind. However, God wanted us to freely choose to love and worship Him because, through obedience, we demonstrate our love for God (John 14:15, 21, 23).

By persuading them to obey him and to disobey God, Satan was successful in causing Adam and Eve to fail God's test. This caused them and their offspring to become servants of Satan through sin unto death (Romans 6:16), which is the wages of sin. But God chose to redeem us by allowing a part of Himself to become man and to pay our death penalties. Jesus is the living Word of God Who became flesh so that He could pay the ultimate price for the redemption of our souls. During His earthly life, Jesus was perfected through obedience to God until He took His last breath. He thereby became the author of eternal salvation unto all who obey Him (Hebrews 5:9). In the end, obedience to God through Jesus Christ is still the only means to the salvation of the saints (Acts 4:10-12).

In John 17:21, Jesus prayed that all of the children of God be one with their triune God; that, just as He and

God are in each other, the children of God be in both
Jesus and God. Jesus, being God incarnate, wanted
nothing more than the realization of God's creative
purpose for us. He prayed that we become both God and
man to the same extent that He is God and man. His
death and resurrection provided the means through
which His prayer could be answered. All who believe
on His ultimate sacrifice for the forgiveness of their
sins, in faith, become children of God. As such, our
triune God lives in us and we in Him. This oneness is
initiated at the very moment of our spiritual rebirths; is
perfected by God over time and is consummated at the
marriage feast of the Lamb. In the world that is to come,
we will neither marry nor be given in marriage to each
other (Luke 20:34-38). We shall all be one through
marriage with Jesus Christ, the second personage of our
triune God. In Revelation 19:7-9, it is written:

> Let us be glad and rejoice, and give honour to
> him: for the marriage of the Lamb is come, and
> his wife hath made herself ready. And to her was
> granted that she should be arrayed in fine linen,
> clean and white: for the fine linen is the
> righteousness of saints. And he saith unto me,
> Write, Blessed are they which are called unto the
> marriage supper of the Lamb. And he saith unto
> me, These are the true sayings of God.

We who are the children of God are the bride of
Christ (2 Corinthians 11:2; Ephesians 5:25), and this
marriage is an eternal union between God's children and
Jesus Christ (Matthew 25:1-13; 1 Thessalonians 4:16-
17). Our collective and individual marriage to Jesus
makes us one with Him (Galatians 3:28), just as a
marriage between a man and a woman causes them to

become one flesh (Genesis 2:24; 1 Corinthians 6:16; Ephesians 5:30-32). It officially completes God's answer to Jesus' prayer that we become one with our triune Godhead (John 17:22).

In His high-priestly prayer, Jesus prayed for the children of God who were given to Him out of the world by God. He did not pray for the world. In this prayer, Jesus stated that we received and believed the words that God gave Him to give to us. Because of this, we are no longer part of the world, just as Jesus is not part of the world; and the world hates us just as it hates Jesus (John 17:5-8, 14, 16).

All of God's children who believe, in faith, the promises of God confess that they are strangers and pilgrims on this earth (Psalm 39:12; Hebrews 11:13). We were separated from this world the moment we were spiritually reborn because the Spirit of Truth lives in us. John 14:17 tells us that the world cannot receive the Spirit of Truth because the world does not see Him nor does it know Him; but we know Him, for He dwells with us and in us. If we were of the world, the world would love us; but we were chosen out of the world, thus we are hated by the world (John 15:18-19). We are therefore instructed in 1 John 2:15-17:

> Love not the world, neither the things that are in the world. If any man love the world, the love of the Father is not in him. For all that is in the world, the lust of the flesh, and the lust of the eyes, and the pride of life, is not of the Father, but is of the world. And the world passeth away, and the lust thereof: but he that doeth the will of God abideth for ever.

Romans 8:1-4 tell us that we are not condemned

because we are in Christ Jesus and walk after the Spirit and not after the flesh. The law of the Spirit of Life in Christ Jesus has freed us from the law of sin and death. For we could never be righteous under the law of the flesh because our sin natures will cause us to inevitably sin. But we are made righteous because God sent His own Son in the likeness of sinful flesh to condemn sin in the flesh for those of us who walk in the Spirit. God will not impose redemption upon us. We have to willingly accept Jesus' sacrifice on our behalf. Paul, therefore, encourages us not to be conformed to this world (Romans 12:2); nor should we worry about worldly things such as what we should eat and drink, as the world does (Luke 12:29-30). Friendship with this world is enmity with God. Whoever loves the world is an enemy of God (James 4:4). That is why the prophet Isaiah tells us, in Isaiah 2:22, that we are to "cease ye from man, whose breath is in his nostrils: for wherein is he to be accounted of?"

The death, burial and resurrection of Jesus Christ resulted in the redemption of all mankind. At that point, the world and Satan were judged, and Satan was doomed to be cast out of heaven unto the earth (John 12:31). Jesus told us that He had to leave so that the Comforter would come and "reprove the world of sin, and of righteousness, and of judgment: of sin, because they believe not on me; of righteousness, because I go to my Father, and ye see me no more; of judgment, because the prince of this world is judged." (John 16:8-11)

We who are not of this world wept when Jesus left, but the world rejoiced. Our sorrow shall be turned into joy (John 16:20). When Jesus left this world, He went to prepare a place for us (John 14:1-4). It is written:

> Eye hath not seen, nor ear heard, neither have
> entered into the heart of man, the things which
> God hath prepared for them that love Him. (1
> Corinthians 2:9)

We *do* know that, as saints (separated holy ones), we shall judge the world and angels, who are ministering spirits sent to minister to the heirs of salvation (Psalm 149:5-9; 1 Corinthians 6:2-3). Jesus tells us that we are not to rejoice in the fact that the spirits are subjected unto us, but rather that our names are written in heaven (Luke 10:20). The fact that we shall rule over all creation sheds immeasurable light on the nature of our oneness with God when we are glorified and raised to our incorruptible states in Christ Jesus. Adam and Eve were given dominion and authority over the earth. Upon our glorification in Jesus, this dominion and authority shall be extended to all physical and spiritual creation. In our current redeemed but corruptible states, we are admonished not to judge anyone lest we be judged by the same measure of judgment meted out by us (Matthew 7:1-11). To do so now would be to condemn ourselves because we all have sinned and come short of the glory of God (Romans 3:23).

Yet when we stand incorruptible and faultless before God through the righteousness of Christ Jesus (Romans 5:21), we will be in a position to judge others, including angels. Through Jesus, Who has washed away our sins with His own blood, we have been made kings and priests unto God, His Father (Revelation 1:5-6). Being kings and priests unto our God, we shall reign with Jesus forever and ever (2 Timothy 2:12; Revelation

5:10; 20:4, 6; 22:5). We will be perfect in all our ways before God, being made sufficient to reign and judge all of creation, a function heretofore exercised only by our triune Godhead but originally intended to be shared with us. Our oneness with God will allow us to share in this awesome responsibility.

We will have incorruptible and immortal bodies (1 Corinthians 15:49-54). As mirror images of Jesus, we shall know the hearts of men (Luke 5:22); travel through matter (John 20:26); appear and disappear at will (Luke 24:36-37); be capable of transfiguration (Matthew 17:1-2); heal all manner of sickness (Matthew 10:1); walk on water (Matthew 14:25-27); have authority over devils (Luke 9:1); raise the dead (John 11:38-44); feed thousands with little or nothing (John 6:5-12); and change water into wine (John 2:1-11). Incredibly, Jesus told us that not only will we be able to do all that He did, but that we will be able to do greater works than these (John 14:12). If only we could fully appreciate the tremendous wonder and significance of our intended roles in God's kingdom, we would run from this world as fast as our feet would carry us straight into the ever-waiting arms of our Lord and Savior, Jesus Christ.

If we keep in mind who we are, Whose we are, and of what world we belong, this present world becomes of no significance to us. All of our efforts would be to seek God's world. It is only when we give up all earthly desires that we obtain the desires of our hearts. It is only when we give up our lives that we gain a more abundant life. It is only when we stop trying to be God that we become one with Him.

Before creation week, God knew that Satan would

succeed in causing Adam and Eve to sin against God. Even though God foreknew that they would choose death instead of life, God elected Adam and Eve, and certain of their offspring who He knew would accept His free gift of eternal salvation, to be restored as heirs to His kingdom and to be holy and conformed to the image of His Son according to His purpose. Their names were written in the Book of Life before the foundation of the world (Ephesians 1:4; 2 Timothy 1:9; Revelation 17:8). Throughout the history of mankind, God has used trials and tribulations to draw His chosen to Himself. For we know that all things work together for good to them that love God and are called according to His purpose (Romans 8:28).

Despite knowing, before creation week, of the fall of man, God did not alter His plan to inhabit and become one with us, His highest creation. Instead, God proceeded with creation week and saw that it was good (Genesis 1:31). We are the center of God's universe, and our fall caused it to slowly die; but God in His infinite grace and mercy secured the restoration of all of physical creation to its original perfection by allowing Himself to become man and die for the sins of all of us. The result of this demonstration of God's unconditional and uncompromising love is the ultimate restoration of Adam, Eve and the chosen among their descendants to our original estate, and the universe to its original order and perfection.

At the end of creation week it was Adam and Eve who had dominion over the earth. They lost that dominion when they sinned against God. Satan, who became one with them through sin, was given authority over the kingdoms of the world through man (Luke 4:6).

Satan was temporarily given this authority despite his own sin against God (Luke 4:5-7; 2 Corinthians 4:4). When Jesus died and was resurrected, Satan's authority was taken from him and given back to mankind through the person of Jesus Christ.

When we praise God for this glorious salvation and ultimate perfect oneness with Him, God inhabits those praises. In Deuteronomy 10:21 it is written: "[God] is thy praise." Psalm 22:3 states: "But thou art holy, O thou that inhabitest the praises of Israel." Should these passages be taken literally? How can God inhabit the praises of His people? In order to answer these questions we must begin with the premise, discussed in earlier chapters, that oneness with God literally means that He lives in His children and His children live in Him. This mutual inhabitation will be perfected when we are glorified and God permanently indwells our future incorruptible bodies. Jesus is our example of this incorruptible eternal oneness with God. When we walk in the Spirit and live in the Spirit (Galatians 5:16, 25), we yield our own desires to those of the Holy Spirit, allowing Him to effectuate His will through us.

Paul tells us to pray "always with all prayer and supplication in the Spirit" (Ephesians 6:18). This means that we are to continuously make prayerful requests, intercessions and praises (1 Timothy 2:1-3). We do not know what we should pray for, or how we should pray, but the Spirit makes intercession for us when we pray (Romans 8:26). How many times have we started a prayer not knowing what to say, only to have the words flow from our mouths as if we had recited a well-rehearsed script. Only the Holy Spirit can do that.

When we pray in the Spirit, the Holy Spirit groans to

God in our stead or inspires our prayers. If God literally prays to Himself for and through us, so, likewise, He praises Himself for and through us. We cannot yet understand why God chooses to use us in this manner. We can only revel in the joy of being used by God in whatever way He sees fit. So let us praise the Lord with all our hearts while His breath of life is still in us because, in doing so, we honor Him by doing what we were created to do. The dead cannot praise God (Psalm 115:17). Indeed, the dead know not anything (Ecclesiastes 9:5).

When God uses each child of His to praise Himself or pray to Himself, the entire Body of Christ collectively manifests itself as the literal voice and Word of God. In Ezekiel 43:2, the prophet describes God's voice as "a sound of many waters." John, in Revelation 14:2, describes a voice he heard from heaven as the "voice of many waters" and as the "voice of a great thunder." Revelation 19:6 tells us that John heard the voice of a great multitude, as the voice of many waters, and as the voice of mighty thunderings, praising God. He also describes Jesus Christ as the Son of Man, whose voice was as the sound of many waters (Revelation 1:15). According to these passages, when God and Jesus Christ speak, their voices are like the sound of many waters. What are the waters that are described here? Revelation 17:1, 15 tell us that "waters" refer to "peoples, and multitudes, and nations, and tongues."

The peoples, multitudes, nations and tongues who compose the voice of Jesus, the Word of God, must be the children of God who compose the Body of Christ. Thus, when Jesus speaks, His voice is "as the sound of many waters," which are the collective praises and prayers of the members of His Body. As Jesus and God are one, and Jesus is the literal voice and Word of God, the same voices that collectively compose the voice of Jesus also collectively compose the voice of God. Since the Holy Spirit inspires all praise (Ephesians 5:18-20) and, indeed, intercedes and makes prayerful praise for and through us (Romans 8:26-27), our praise and worship of God is initiated by God our Father, inspired by the Holy Spirit, and spoken collectively by and through us through the personage of Jesus Christ, who is the Word of God. The words we speak while in this complete state of mutual inhabitation and oneness with God have the living, faithful power of God in them. All that we speak in faith, individually and collectively, will be realized because God lives in these words and, consequently, inhabits our inspired praises and prayers.

Before his fall, Adam had the living power of God in his voice. When he named every living creature on the earth, that was the name thereof (Genesis 2:19-20). After Adam's fall, God no longer inhabited his words. Consequently, before the death and resurrection of God through Jesus Christ, only men of God who were anointed with the Holy Spirit had the power of God in the words they spoke. For instance, because he spoke in faith through the Spirit that was upon him, Elijah was able to speak fire from heaven to kill the king's men pursuing him (2 Kings 1:9-15). Isaac could not take back his blessings upon his sons Jacob and Esau because, being anointed with the Spirit, his spoken words were true, faithful and sure (Genesis 27:30-39). However, the power exhibited by these anointed Old Testament men of God was from without, temporary and exceptional. They could be led by the Spirit (Luke 2:27), but they could not be filled with the Holy Spirit because they were not spiritually born again with the Holy Spirit. Therefore the Holy Spirit did not indwell them. In Old Testament times, the Holy Spirit could only come upon them and anoint them with His power.

It wasn't until the ascension of Jesus that the Holy Spirit indwelt mankind, and the power of God lives in and through us. Jesus, as the only begotten Son of God and the head of the Body of Christ, was the first to be permanently filled with the Holy Spirit (Luke 4:1). His state of perfect oneness with God necessitated that whatever He asked of God would be given unto Him. For instance, Jesus asked God the Father to raise Lazarus from the dead. Because Jesus is in the Father and the Father in Him, Jesus' prayer was granted, and Lazarus rose from the dead (John 11:17-46). After God's ultimate sacrifice for the forgiveness of sins, anyone who in faith believes on the name of Jesus Christ abides in God and God in him; therefore that person can ask anything of God and He will do it (John 14:12-14; 15:16; 16:23-24). We are limited only by the extent of our faith.

In these passages from the Gospel of John, the phrase "in my name" literally means "as My agent." This type of agency is unique because the agent and the One the agent represents indwell each other so much so that they both carry the same name. The agent therefore speaks with the authority and power of God. When we ask of God "in His name," as we have just defined that phrase, God will grant us our prayers because in essence He is granting prayers He has inspired us to pray.

Jesus gave His disciples power and authority over all devils and to cure diseases (Luke 9:1-2). Jesus tells us, in Matthew 17:19-21, that faith, with prayer and fasting, can cast out demons. The spiritually reborn person has the power to do all things through Christ Jesus, if he abides in Jesus and asks in faith, wavering not (James 1:5-6). This is so because the power demonstrated by the Spirit-filled children of God is from within, permanent and normal (i.e., from God).

Bishop Clifford M. Johnson, Jr., who graciously wrote the Foreword to this book and who serves as my Pastor at Mount Pleasant Church and Ministries, has been teaching us about a concept he calls "the principle of equivalent effect". It relates to the immutability of God; in other words, the unchanging nature of God. Therefore, if, upon a fervent request, God responded a certain way in the past, He must do so again for us. The Holy Scriptures are replete with instances where God answered the prayers of His people; many times miraculously. Because God does not favor any one person over another and cannot change, what He does for one He has to do for all. To the extent that we beseech Him to do anything He has already done in the past in response to similar prayerful requests, we can rest assured that He will respond to our requests in a like manner. Because of His immutability, it is impossible for God to do anything other than generate a result which is equivalent to His past conduct. Since He has delivered, fed, saved, healed, empowered, inspired, blessed and talked to His own in the past, the principle of equivalent effect tells us that we can live in the confidence that He will do the same for us.

The fulfillment of God's master plan for the restoration of all who will choose His free gift of eternal life instead of eternal death and damnation will be a testament to the consistency of His purpose and the reliability of His promises. We will be returned to our originally created estate in the image of Jesus because God cannot do anything but be truthful to His Word. If we ask to be saved, we will be saved. In response to Jesus' prayerful request, we will be given incorruptible bodies that will house God Himself and in and through which God will exercise His dominion over all creation. We will possess all of the attributes, characteristics and power of God and therefore will be uniquely capable of being utilized by God in this fashion. God's unchanging nature provides God no other option then to answer Jesus' prayer.

Having these Godly qualities is not something that we should take lightly or acknowledge with halfhearted indifference. Satan and the rest of the fallen angels chose to rebel against God and suffer eternal damnation because they lacked such qualities. All that Jesus is we shall become. The significance of that statement cannot be overstated. We shall possess all of the treasures in the Kingdom of God. To be given the honor and privilege of wielding the power of God would be too much for us to handle if we did not possess the attributes and characteristics of God. We were created to be one with God as a direct result of the limitless love and mercy of our Father, Who was willing to share Himself with His highest creation by creating us to also have limitless love and mercy being made in His image and after His likeness.

We do not have to wait until our earthly lives end for us to experience this miraculous oneness with the Almighty. There are many instances in the Holy Scriptures in which men and women of God enjoyed deep personal relationships with God. On two such occasions, the relationship between man and God was so intimate that God took them up to heaven without them ever tasting physical death. One such relationship was that of Enoch, who was translated into heaven (Genesis 5:21-24). The Hebrew verb and preposition used to denote his "walk with God" signifies "to live in intimacy with God." The Hebrew word used for "translated" is the same word used in chapter 2 of 2 Kings when Elijah was translated into heaven without tasting death. Even though the Holy Spirit did not indwell them, both of these men experienced a oneness with God that most of us will only enjoy in eternity with God. Their anointing was so heavy that whatever they asked for was done unto them. We can attain this same degree of intimacy with God during our lifetimes if we give up all personal desires and interests and let God be our everything in and through us.

Our spiritual rebirths begin our individual and collective intimate walks with God. The Holy Spirit searches all things, including the deep things of God; and as our spiritual walks with God progress He reveals these things to us (1 Corinthians 2:10). Our knowledge and understanding of God will grow to levels heretofore incomprehensible. There is no limit to God, and therefore there is no limit to our knowledge and understanding of God. Our growth in Him will be eternal in nature and substance.

Praise be to God for His perfect will and our role in it. We thank God not for what we will obtain as a result of our union with Him, but because He loved us so much that He allows us to serve Him in this way despite our sin of disobedience. He mercifully redeemed us unto Himself by allowing a part of Himself to become one of us and suffer an undeserved temporary, physical and spiritual death.

God said: "Let us make man in our image, after our likeness." Despite the best efforts of Satan and man, nothing could be done to cause these words to return to God void. It is written in Isaiah:

> Yea, I have spoken it, I will also bring it to pass; I have purposed it, I will also do it. (Isaiah 46:11) So shall my word be that goeth forth out of my mouth: it shall not return unto me void, but it shall accomplish that which I please, and it shall prosper in the thing whereto I sent it. (Isaiah 55:11)

The Holy Scriptures are replete with prophecies of the Messiah being fulfilled in Jesus the Christ. Since these inspired words of God shall not return to Him void, nothing could have stopped Jesus, Who is the living Word of God, from completing His mission for the salvation of souls. We can take comfort in the knowledge that Jesus' faithful prayer that we be one with our triune Godhead will likewise not return to Him void. We shall be completely conformed to the image and likeness of God, through Jesus Christ, and enjoy the experience of being God and man as brethren of Jesus Christ, as was originally intended.

Grace and peace be multiplied unto you through the knowledge of God, and of Jesus our Lord, According as his divine power hath given unto us all things that pertain unto life and godliness, through the knowledge of him that hath called us to glory and virtue: Whereby are given unto us exceeding great and precious promises: that by these ye might be partakers of the divine nature, having escaped the corruption that is in the world through lust. (2 Peter 1:2-4)

ABOUT THE AUTHOR

Born in Baltimore, Maryland, Ronald E. Richardson is a senior attorney with the law offices of Peter G. Angelos, P.C. where, for the past twenty years, he has specialized in various forms of products liability and personal injury litigation.

Mr. Richardson obtained B.S. and M.S. degrees in criminal justice from Northeastern University in Boston, and a J.D. degree from Loyola Law School in Los Angeles.

He is spiritually and professionally active in his community, serving in prayer ministries, in mentorship programs and on various boards and committees. He is a former chair of the deacon board of Bel Forest Baptist Church and presently attends Mt. Pleasant Church and Ministries.

A certified NFL agent, Mr. Richardson has also assisted in the production of two documentary films: *Color at the Bar* and *Maryland State Bar Association: An Oral History*.

He is married to Ella Richardson and they have two children.